358.4

Guyton, Boone T.
Air Base

17855

Carnegie Public Library
Robinson, Illinois

AIR BASE

North Island—home to many a naval aviator.

(Official Photograph, U. S. Navy.)

Air Base

by

BOONE T. GUYTON
*Test Pilot,
Vought-Sikorsky Aircraft*

New York WHITTLESEY HOUSE *London*
McGRAW-HILL BOOK COMPANY, INC.

AIR BASE

Copyright, 1941, *by the* McGraw-Hill Book Company, Inc.

All rights reserved. This book, or parts thereof, may not be reproduced in any form without permission of the publishers.

SECOND PRINTING

PUBLISHED BY WHITTLESEY HOUSE
A division of the McGraw-Hill Book Company, Inc.

Printed in the United States of America by the Maple Press Co., York, Pa.

To

THE UNITED STATES NAVAL AIR FORCE
WHOSE FLIERS, OFFICERS AND MEN
ARE MOLDING AMERICA'S FIRST
LINE OF DEFENSE

Acknowledgment

I WISH to acknowledge editorial help to Russell Owen, of the *New York Times*, and I am indebted to the following for research help and checking of facts: Charles Gale, Editor, *The Sportsman Pilot;* The Bureau of Navigation, Department of the Navy; Lt. Comdr., C. S. Alexander, U.S.N.; Lieutenant Ben Scott Custer, U.S.N.; Lieutenant (j.g.) W. W. Moss, U.S.N.R.

I want to thank the *American Magazine* for lending me a picture, and Miss Emily Darling, of Vought-Sikorsky Aircraft, for assistance in preparing the manuscript for the press.

BOONE T. GUYTON.

Contents

Acknowledgment	vii
Chapter I	3
Chapter II	12
Chapter III	27
Chapter IV	46
Chapter V	65
Chapter VI	83
Chapter VII	101
Chapter VIII	119
Chapter IX	136
Chapter X	158
Chapter XI	189
Chapter XII	223
Chapter XIII	257
Index	285

Note for the Second Printing, Dec. 17, 1941

Now that the war has come to the Western Hemisphere, the Navy is in the thick of battle, and already it has been proved that capital ships can and will be sunk by aircraft. Again, the bases from which the forces of both air arms operate have come to the force and their importance is doubly stressed. Movements of fleet and army hinge on those outposts which carry both the provision for the attack, and yes, the brunt of the attack itself. For already these famous words are spoken as the air bases clear their decks—"Remember Pearl Harbor!"

BOONE T. GUYTON.

AIR BASE

Chapter I

THE crash siren started up out of nowhere, wailed out into the night. It hit high pitch just about the time I had kicked off my last shoe and pulled on my pajamas for an eight-hour hop into dreamland. As I crawled back out of bed, jerked on trousers and sneaks, I thought to myself, this San Diego howler sounds just like the old one back at Pensacola. It brought the same results. There was a scuffle of scraping feet and slamming doors, some hurried talk with a few wisecracks. "Some green-eared ensign probably ground-looped out on the field." "It's my crib, and don't stack the cards before we get back."

Basil Alexander Martin, Jr., stuck his head around the corner. "Who the hell you suppose did this one?" he said in about the same tone I had listened to for a year back in training. Bud never did get very excited about anything. As we hit the bottom step a head thrust through the screen door. "Everybody with a car get down to South Beach. One of Scouting Two's planes went in off the breakwater and didn't have time to drop a flare. We need a lot of lights." The head disappeared.

Outside the officers' quarters we crawled into "Hotdamn," our rolling bucket of bolts. Cars were already streaming out toward the beach, and we fell into line. Landing planes came in one after another out of the black across Spanish Bight, then into the glare of the field floods, and sat down on the black tar, throwing long, fast shadows. The tires screeched and grump-grumped above the howling siren. A white flare was burning vividly out in the middle of the black landing mat, and we knew from training days that this was the recall signal for all planes still in the air. (It isn't healthy for two or three planes to try circling around in the dark looking for a proverbial needle in the haystack. The danger of collision at night is quadrupled in the air, and base radio had probably already called all ships back to the field supplementing the flare.)

We went down past the last squadron hangar,

around the corner back of the big balloon hangar, and by the rows of squatty stucco houses that bounded South Field. As we passed the officers' club, a security watch officer pointed down to the edge of the water, where cars were pulling up into line, throwing their light beams up high. "Follow the last car, and get your lights on the water." Bud pulled "Hotdamn" up alongside the station fire truck, whose big spotlight was playing out across the black Pacific Ocean. I kept wondering who had gone in and whether it could have been one of our class—Kelley, Jones, MacKrille. They had gone to Scouting Two, but surely they couldn't be night-flying yet. We had arrived on the base only this evening, and Bud and I had been among the first to get orders to a carrier squadron based at North Island.

Up and down the white sand beach a motley crowd of officers, enlisted men, and even some women in evening clothes were scanning the inky surf for signs of a rubber life raft that would spell O.K. in their language. I've found it the same everywhere. Aboard a naval base—a small world in itself—the call goes out for help, and the shipmate who is in trouble gets it. From the third-class light, and out of the blackness came one, two, three parachute flares, lighting the water for several miles. The Grumman kept circling overhead. Half an hour. People were slowly registering that hopeless look as the minutes passed. No one left.

"There he blows!" The big chief mechanic on the fire engine bellowed out lustily, pointing down the beach. We started running and had almost made the spot when two wet figures jumped out of the little rubber raft and dragged it up on the sand. A big cheer went up and down the beach, and I would have given a lot to have had a camera and got a movie of that dramatic setting. Neither Blackburn nor his mechanic was hurt any, but they were wet and shivering.

"Rowed in from about half a mile out," Blackburn said, wiping water from his face and eyes. "Plane sank almost immediately, and we just did get the boat out. Boy, these lights sure helped on the beach. The haze offshore is pretty thick."

The crowd backed away to let them through, and before we could offer congratulations the station "meat wagon" (our crude term for ambulance) was hauling them off for a good rubdown and medical check. I thought what a lucky couple of boys they were to get away with an emergency landing at night without even the help of a landing light or flare. That water looked awfully black.

Then I thought back to the time Jimmy Abraham had landed at night in Pensacola with one wheel hung up in the belly of his plane. We were about as green about flying then as we were about service aviation now. I'll never forget how we lined the runway at Corry Field that night, wishing so hard for old Jim that the wheel should have freed itself. He did a good job, though. When the plane nosed over and ended up on its back, Jim came out from under it with just a slight change in his profile. He now packs a beautiful Roman nose.

We found out that the flotation bags had worked on Blackburn's plane but that the landing was pretty hard, and one bag had carried away before they had been able to get the life raft out. The plane had sunk shortly after, but they could see the lights of the cars lined up on the beach, so they had proceeded to paddle in. Uncle Sam was happy. A plane worth a few thousand dollars is nothing compared to the lives of pilot and mechanic. Once you have been through the Navy flight training, you never forget the sentence, "We can always buy another *airplane*." You don't buy pilots.

Back at the quarters, I crawled into the bunk once more. Downstairs the boys were still talking over the night's occurrence, reiterating last week's "close one," and carrying on with some first-class hanger talk. But we had had enough for our first day aboard the base. I lay there, thinking back about a week before, when down at Pensacola the captain had issued his last admonition to his departing flock. We had stood beaming, at attention, gold wings secured on white uniforms, orders in hand.

" . . . and remember, gentlemen. When you get out to your squadrons in the fleet, Uncle Sam is putting you in commission like a new battleship. You are going out with a year of hard flight training behind you and a pair of wings. It is up to you to maintain the high standard set up by the Naval Air Force and to perform your mission to the best of your ability. Congratulations and good luck."

That was all. We had shoved off, scampered across the country, and reported in to the officer of the day, Naval Air Station at North Island, San Diego, California. I kept remembering how often I had heard those phrases, "Now, when you get out to the fleet . . . when you get out in an operating squadron . . . !" We used to spend whole nights listening to the officers who had just come back from fleet duty tell about their experiences—how it felt to land aboard a carrier for the first time, what an operating squadron did, and how little we would actually know about flying until we had been through a couple of months of fleet duty.

Well, we were here—green, gawking, and self-conscious. But we were here and ready to have a mechanic paint our name across the fuselage of the ship we were to fly with the squadron. There was one thing about it. Action was spelled with capital letters out here, and there would be plenty of flying and a lot happening, both good and bad. By the end of the week our whole class of forty-two would report in, and I had already heard rumors of a party coming up at the officers' club as a sort of initial icebreaker and get-together. I fell asleep, wondering what the new squadron would be like, whether the skipper—the old man—was hard-boiled or "just one of the boys" and whether the squadron was doing gunnery or bombing exercises. Dive-bombing Squadron Two off the carrier *Lexington* had held the annual fleet record for dive bombing several times. I hoped I still had my batting eye.

Chapter II

"Mr. Guyton, may I have your orders?" the yeoman in the squadron office asked me, as I stood gaping at the pictures surrounding the long green table in the other room, somewhat overawed at these new surroundings. What I had expected to find on first entering a squadron ready room I don't remember. I do remember that we had heard so much talk about "no romance in the fleet" and the like that we had leaned over backward from any of the glamour the movies had portrayed. Now I was looking at the walls of the "High Hatters," the hot bombing outfit of the fleet, and the first impression was not quite so drab or uninteresting as the boys had depicted. I turned my orders over to the yeoman and went back to surveying my future home.

The long ready room was lined with chairs that

surrounded the counsel table. Above them on the walls were pictures of formations, carriers, dogfights, and former officers of the unit. A big squadron flight board that hung at one end of the room by the coffee mess was covered with schedules of the day's and week's operations. Six small rooms opened out of the ready room, and the signs above the doors told the story—Flight, Navigation, Radio and Communications, Engineering, Captain, Executive Officer. It doesn't take long to learn what each one of these divisions means and what specific duty each performs. You soon realize that a complete squadron of eighteen planes is organized, drilled, run, and kept in top shape right here.

Outside, the usual early morning ground fog was fast burning off.

"The squadron officers will be here any minute, sir," the yeoman told me. "We muster at eight." I looked at my watch and realized that in my eagerness I had arrived early. The coffee mess at the far corner of the room was already bubbling hard. (In the Navy coffee is as important a part of any ready room as wings to an airplane. I don't see how a naval aviator can fly without it.) As I nosed around the room I wondered how Bud was doing up at his squadron, Marine Fighting Two.

"McClure is my name. Glad to know you." We made the rounds. "Kane, Williams, Nuessle, Stephens. This is Ensign Guyton, gentlemen, just reporting in from Pensacola." I was thinking that they could all tell that. My uniform, with its new shiny brass and bright gold wings stood out like a sore thumb among the salt-dulled braid of the older officers. It is the first distinction between newcomer and old-timer in the fleet. McClure, who I learned was flight officer, finished the introductions, and then we went in to see the skipper.

"Glad to have you aboard, Guyton. Draw up a chair." I liked Commander Alexander from the start. He was a weather-beaten, rugged-looking gentleman, who looked as though he could handle any situation with cool precision. Well liked, usually called "Alex," even by the junior officers, the skipper was one of the smoothest flyers in the squadron.

"Have you had your physical?" he said. I told him I hadn't. "Well, you had best go right up to sick bay now and get it squared away. We are up to fly record bombing next week, and the rule is that every member of the squadron will fly. That means that you won't have much time to practice, but we won't expect any miracles. Just do the best you can." This was the type of man for whom you felt like doing your utmost. Some men have the knack of leading, and some fall short. But old Alex was my idea of a born leader. I certainly hoped I could get some hits.

"Now, as for the squadron," he went on. "Your job, outside of flying, will be assistant engineering officer under Lieutenant Nuessle. He will show you the ropes. You've been assigned Number Eighteen in the squadron, and Nuessle leads that section. If there is anything you don't understand about what is going on here ask any of the officers, and they will be glad to give you a hand."

He smiled, and I went out. There was a man I could really fly for, and Uncle Sam was fortunate to have commanding officers like him.

That was my welcome to the squadron. Before evening I had been to sick bay and passed a physical, met the rest of the squadron officers, and read the flight rules for North Island and the outlying fields.

The immediate outlying fields around an air base

are nearly as important as the main flying field on the base. It is to these that you go to practice stationary-target dive bombing, carrier-landing practice (primary fieldwork), and such various activities as scouting exercises, rendezvous for mock warfare and battle practice, and familiarization in new types of aircraft. Several days later, when I had a chance to fly around to see these fields, I began to realize the military importance of such auxiliary points in time of actual warfare. When it was known when the attack would reach the base (by means of long-range patrol boats and scouting planes) all the squadrons could be flown to designated auxiliary fields. Here they would simply wait—or take part in defending the base—until the attack was over, leaving nothing but a blank landing field, with its surrounding shops, for the enemy to bomb.

Both the major belligerents of the present war are using this method so successfully that neither has sustained any heavy losses of aircraft destroyed on the home base. I had the list well in mind. Border Field, down Mexico way; Otay, cut out like a patch from the heart of sprawling Otay Mesa; Oceanside, on the coast toward Los Angeles; San

Marcos, in the green, grassy valley of San Marcos River; Ocatilla, lying in the blistering heat of the Imperial Desert across the high range of Lagunas. Each had its circle target of white stones laid out at one end, and I was to look down my sights many times at those rings while trying to get steady in a dive for a bull's-eye. You can't foresee those days when you will be practicing dive bombing at one of these fields and suddenly have to land to help pull a broken shipmate from the wreckage of his plane because "something went wrong" and he didn't pull out. It is good that you can't.

The next afternoon I climbed into flight gear for my first squadron flight and gathered around the ready-room table with the rest of the squadron for last-minute instructions. You feel just a little proud sitting there with seventeen old-timers, ready to take off on a mission and waiting for the captain of the "team" to come out and issue the last-minute dope. I was still mentally munching a sandwich of course rules, air battle force instructions, and other pertinent information when the captain came in.

"We climb to twelve thousand ahead and south of the horizontal bombers. When we pick up the ship that is to be heading north just above the Coronados Islands I'll put you in echelon." The captain never minced words. Our orders came through to dive-bomb the radio-controlled *Utah*, a stately old battleship of yesteryear, and we were about set. This was just one of the long lines of "conferences" you took part in before squadron flights. They occur almost daily for the obvious reason of "dope delivering"—instructions and information, to be more formal. "The second division will close up on the first. I'd like to cut our attack time down, which means nose-to-cut tail diving. Any questions?"

"Where do we rendezvous after the attack, captain?" I looked down the table at him, past the seventeen old-timers, as I spoke, self-conscious as a bush-league shortstop in his first big game.

"Inboard toward the coast at two thousand. You are flying Number Eighteen, Guyton. When you have finished your dive, call on the radio, and advise the squadron following us that we have completed our attack. All right, let's go. And remember —we want some hits."

You expect this direct and unadulterated lingo when you get set in the fleet, for time is of prime importance. Your job is handed you over that long green-covered table in the ready room, and when you crawl into your cockpit the ensuing split-second timing is a matter of using what God gave you and the Navy has developed—some brains! An air base that operates fourteen squadrons of planes on a single mission needs coordination as fine and precise as gears of a watch. Minutes are long intervals. Seconds are cut.

Out on the line in front of the long rows of hangars eighteen Vought dive bombers were warming up, bombs hung in place, and mechanics were giving a last swipe at telescope sights. Just twenty minutes later and we were to be in position to attack—nose to tail! As I buckled my safety belt and plugged in my earphones I began to wonder, but not for long. Lyons, our line chief, gave the signal. Chocks were pulled free, and we taxied out, swung into three plane sections, and waited. Down the line of heads the skipper's hand went up, followed by the section leaders in order, until all were set. We started to roll and, seconds later, picked up our wheels, slid over into division formations of three sections each, and climbed.

At twelve thousand we leveled off, swung out

into an echelon, and closed up. I gazed down over the wing to the water far below. There, where Point Loma prodded out into the ocean, was the old Spanish lighthouse, the point at which Cabrillo had landed from a galleon way back in 1542. I wondered what he would think if he could see a hundred airplanes roaring overhead today instead of the lazy gulls he probably watched.

Way back from the tail of the squadron, I could see the skipper's plane start an easy turn toward the islands, and halfway across the solid blue stretch of sea I picked up a white spreading wake. We were going in with the afternoon sun at our backs. The radio cracked.

"Bombing Two, attack—attack!"

I picked up some little white spurts of spray around the battle wagon far below and knew that we were going in right under the last section of horizontal bombers and that those were bomb splashes. Great!

There is a certain unexplainable feeling that you absorb from this bombing business. It is a sensation that says, "I won't get hit; nothing can touch me," which takes charge of you as you look down at the target far below. You get the itch to stick the nose down, put the power on, and scream like a mammoth hawk at that seemingly defenseless little play boat bouncing along through the seas. The lack of a ground sensation of terrific speed plays its part, and just sitting there in the cockpit with a thousand horsepower at your finger tips provides a fanatical assurance that "you can't get hurt." It usually takes a proverbial "close shave" to make a pilot realize exactly what can happen and does happen. How many of the young pilots with their meager two or three hundred hours of flying experience have had their overconfidence blasted into the hereafter in the present war overseas before they realized what *could* happen!

I checked instruments and ran over the diving checkoff list. Cowl flaps, landing flaps, wheels up, arming wire, sight open, seat down, high pitch. All set. It was follow-the-leader now, and I was one of the "High Hats." I began to have a sneaking suspicion that the wet place behind my ears was supposed to be there.

Number One peeled off and started down, followed in a pouring movement by Two, Three, and Four. In the rippling wing over I caught the flash of silver wings as the planes ahead rolled. Through the telescope sight I watched the tail and stubby back of Number Seventeen as I hung on his slip stream, wondering if everything was O.K. There he went, up and over. I hauled back and rolled right behind him, my propeller as close to his tail as I dared put it. The nose dropped down, down, straight at the tiny white target. Through the sight I counted six planes diving straight at the water and, far below, three or four pulling out in a rounded arc.

The air speed jumped to two hundred, two forty, three hundred, and the altimeter started to unwind. The tiny speck on the water—superstructure, stacks, and guns—grew fast as more and more white splashes encircled it. Seven thousand, six, four. My hand slid up to the bomb release. The wind got that moaning yet whistling shriek, and I crouched as low as possible into the cockpit behind the windshield. Three thousand—and time to get out. I jerked the handle and pulled back on the stick, still tailing the plane ahead.

Ship, water, plane, and horizon started to merge into gray, gray almost black, and I knew I had pulled out too fast, that the weight I felt was not

(Official Photograph, U. S. Navy.)

Famous Vought dive bombers—a section in echelon formation ready to attack.

(Facing page 22)

enlisted man in his barracks, to the admiral in his spacious quarters, the aid gathers as a family. White dinner jackets mingled with green uniforms, blue denims and half and half pajamas with service blues. Within twenty minutes a hundred cars had assembled along the shore line, and groups of people walked the beach, straining into the damp night for a Very signal or some sign from the occupants of the disabled plane. By now the last plane had landed on the field, and the silence was broken only by lapping waves and hushed talk.

Bud had come back from talking to one of Scouting Two's pilots who had been flying. "It was Blackburn and one of the radio men. His engine cut on his final approach to the field, and he landed out about a thousand yards from the beach. He was too low to use his radio or flares. The ready plane standing by at the ramp is having some trouble getting started."

Even as he spoke you could hear the unmistakable growl of the Grumman amphibian taking off from the bay on the other side of the island. A short few minutes later and he was circling over us, out to sea, his green and red running lights dipping down toward the water. Then on went the landing

three trucks on top of me but gravity getting in her lick. I swore—not in pain but in aggravation. It was black all around. Then the gray came back, the strain eased off, and as the horizon came into the ring cowl I saw several of our planes rendezvoused off toward the shore line.

The water a thousand feet below was going by in a blur as I reached for the microphone. "Bombing Two—attack completed." The squadron was well joined up, circling lazily, waiting on little me before I could catch them, and it seemed that even the wings of my plane must be turning a bright shade of green. On the way back Neussle, my section leader, turned around and grinned. I felt better then, though I had no idea where my bomb had landed. I wiped the oil smudges off my goggles and stored up for future use the experience of too fast a pull-out.

Back at the squadron we filed into the ready room, pulling off helmets and gloves, and, with coffee and cigarettes, sat down around the table to await the captain's verdict.

"Joe, you corkscrewed all the way down on that one." Vensel, assistant flight officer, grinned. "Aw, the sun was too hot on my back. Did we get any hits?" "Couldn't tell, but the skipper came awful close." Vensel, I found, was the spark plug of the outfit. He was small and jovial and because of his egg-shaped head and pint size was always being chided in good spirit by the boys. The skipper came in.

"Gentlemen, that was very good. We only got five hits, but our bomb pattern was good, and the results look promising. The dive time was good, but I would still like to cut it shorter. We are scheduled for the eight o'clock hop in the morning. Any questions?" There was none. "That's all. You may secure for the day."

I wondered why he didn't warn me about the pull-out and mention the time I cost the squadron by joining up late. But that was the way with Alex. He knew that you learn this business and its tricks by a little experience and that he had once come out of Pensacola to an air base for the first time, as tender as the rest. He probably knew, too, that I had learned a lesson. I had.

Bud had a lot to say that night. He had started in up at the Marine Corps squadron, flying a scouting problem that had taken them well below the Mexican border out to sea to locate an "enemy" destroyer. They had found it and got back to land just before dark. The Marine Corps held down the east side of the field, and their four squadrons, fighting, scouting, and two bombing squadrons, were stationed close to the big balloon hangar, somewhat apart from the Navy squadrons, yet working in conjunction with the fleet.

The Marine organization is a part of the Navy, it is true, but the spirit of the corps has always been so high and its accomplishments so outstanding that it is popularly regarded as sufficient unto itself. Servicemen, both Army and Navy, unstintingly and quite naturally recognize this unusual condition. They should! For the marines have emerged from wars of the past with the reputation of being the toughest, fightingest organization ashore or afloat. While ashore, one of the duties of the Marine detachment is the major part of policing the establishment and keeping orders and regulations obeyed. Doing this job just as well as they do their many other jobs has brought the marines in for a lot of legpulling by their brothers in service. But they can take it!

As we sat there boasting Navy over Marine Corps and vice versa, the last three fellows of our class from Pensacola came in. They were full of the latest happenings back there, of how orders for the next class were coming through to battleships and cruisers and who cracked up at Corry Field the day they shoved off. All this seemed far away now. In fact, it was kindergarten stuff, so it seemed, and all a part of the dim past. We had been out in the fleet less than a week—and less than two weeks away from Pensacola! We felt we were in the big league now. This fleet business wasn't play or instruction any more. It was all in dead earnest. This was operating from Uncle Sam's front line, from his biggest air base, and we just couldn't get excited about the old training station any more. Bud tried to send the newcomers off to bed.

"O.K., tenderfeet," he said with the put-on older brother tone in his voice. "We've had a hard day, and it's time to hit the bunk." You should have seen the looks of surprised disgust that shadowed the faces of the newcomers. Then they climbed Bud's ample frame and worked him over in good old Navy fashion. Like a typical marine he wouldn't say "uncle."

Chapter III

You can't just call North Island an island and let it go at that—primarily because it isn't an island. If you drove across from San Diego, you would board a ferryboat, cross the bay between hurrying destroyers and cruisers, and drive out into the little town of Coronado. More than seven-tenths of this quiet little resort is taken up with the homes of the naval officers from the air station, who have only to drive across Spanish Bight, a backwash from the bay, in order to be on the base. Here, along the palm-bordered streets, Navy wives stop to chat and discuss the affairs of Navy life as only Navy wives can. Along the sand beaches and on the tennis courts, Navy juniors romp—amid the roar of "daddy's squadron coming up the strand."

Surrounding the "Island" are the bay, the Pacific Ocean, and the bight, which backs up along its eastern side. The south shore of North Island, however, continues a narrow strip of sand closing the gap between bay and ocean and runs on down southward past Coronado to the border of Mexico, some sixteen miles below. The Silver Strand, as it is called, is only two or three hundred yards wide, holding South Bay from the Ocean and rounding out into the mainland at the bay's lower end. Principally because of the strategic importance of this defendable land location and the well-protected bay that berths destroyers, cruisers, and carriers, the Navy has constructed its busiest air station here. It is one of the busiest flying fields in the world. One day, as I was thumbing through an old magazine, I found its interesting history, which is typical of the histories of many of the huge bases now being set up for operations in connection with defense of the Western Hemisphere.

Like many of our important flying centers, this base started as a commercial project. Since 1913 the Army had been active here, but since 1917 the Navy had known that this was the spot from which to eye all points west. Old Rockwell Field (the southern part of North Island) was the original nest of a host of Army pilots. By 1938 the Navy

AIR BASE

was occupying the last hangar of the tan-colored squadrons and now is sole proprietor—after the Army was moved to Sunnyvale up near San Francisco.

The original Navy detachment possessed three planes that made use of this site. The year was 1912, and naval aviation was in its infancy. Short, noisy, and dangerous were the flights carried out from the one runway through the sagebrush and from the calm waters of Spanish Bight. The previous year Glenn Curtiss had made the first seaplane flight in the world from the bight, a feat that is commemorated by a plaque in front of the base administration building. Yes, those were great days in aviation. Imagine the contrast between those three rattling, shaky, outrigger planes and the hundreds of roaring fighters, bombers, and patrol planes that now fly daily out of field and bay to accomplish their missions.

In 1917 Lieutenant E. W. Spencer of the United States Navy was detailed to establish and command a naval air station on North Island. His instructions were to establish "(*a*) a flight school, (*b*) a school for mechanics, and (*c*) a coast patrol department." These orders he carried out and, in addition, laid plans for permanent buildings to take the place of the temporary ramshackle ones he was forced to use.

In 1921 the whole Pacific air force was based on North Island. It consisted, in all, of thirty-six airplanes, an assortment of seaplanes, torpedo planes, and one lonesome bomber. But time and advancement go hand in hand, with neither waiting long for the other. On May 10, 1927, Charles A. Lindbergh lifted the "Spirit of St. Louis" from the field for his fifteen-hour flight to St. Louis, then flew on to New York, Paris, and fame. You will remember the mass nonstop flights of the patrol planes to Hawaii and the Canal Zone in the last few years. Then, recently, a squadron of eighteen took off from the bay as hundreds of wives lined the shore to wave good-by—and landed a short time later in Sitka, Alaska! But there is more to a hard flying base than simply the squadrons and their flight operations. I soon found it out.

Early one morning, less than a week after I had first arrived, the engineering officer thought up an idea for which I, his assistant, was grateful.

"You had better take the day off and make the rounds of the station to see where everything is located. We'll have our hands full next month, getting the planes squared away for the big cruise, and you'll save a lot of time if you know beforehand where to get things done on the station." Then he gave me a slip of paper listing where to start and how to make a thorough inspection of shops, hangars, and repair buildings. A big air base is similar to an aircraft carrier. If you don't know the tricks of getting around in its maze of shops, storerooms, and hangars, you need a guide.

"I'll see that you are left off the flight schedule today," he said. I took the slip and started out. On the field, planes had already begun to take off for the first flight of the day.

The low stucco overhaul shops were churning with work. More than half of the Navy's fleet of service aircraft received their major overhauling here, and I realized again that what we did in our own squadron hangar was simply the minor upkeep. Under the roofs of these overhaul shops you find the most modern equipment for repairing everything from the tiniest and most sensitive instrument to the giant patrol boats. Long rows of engines are constantly being assembled and disassembled, checked over, and made new for another several hundred hours of flying.

You sit behind your howling power plant for hours upon endless hours, driving it through wind, snow, and salt spray, imposing terrific speeds on its intricate crankshaft and gears in dives and dogfights. All during these several hundred hours your mechanic has nursed it along, kept a watchful eye on its vital parts, checked it every few hours. But finally it reaches the point where care and checks no longer keep it in top shape. Then out of the plane it comes, and up to the end of the major overhaul line.

As I stood and observed the procedure it became clear. At one end of the overhaul line the engine is dismantled on its special stand, its integral parts taken to remote sections of the shop for cleaning, spraying, painting. As the stand moves, so does the engine. Back come the parts, assembly begins, and several hours later a completely overhauled and freshly painted power plant is ready for its test-stand run-in. Back it goes to the squadron, ready for several hundred more hours of flying. I went up to the second floor, where all the aircraft instruments are repaired, adjusted, and calibrated. Here was the place to come for any engine or instrument information for the squadron. Before we finally got aboard the carrier for the start of the big cruise I had spent many hours rushing back and forth between the hangar and this shop, finding out when an engine would be finished, signing papers for the one just delivered, or exchanging an air-speed indicator that had "got tired."

I crossed the street back of the balloon hangar, passed the Marine squadron, and went into the fuselage and wing shop. The place was full of skeleton fuselages, wings, tail surfaces—some half covered—all being worked on. At one end of the building I found a group of men stripping a seemingly good airplane.

"Trouble?" I asked, with as nonstupid a ring to the question as possible. The enlisted man looked up, talking as he worked. "Yes, sir. This was Scouting Two's plane that went in the water the other evening. The *Mary Ann* hoisted it up after a diver located it." I was mystified. He went on. "We should have it overhauled and flying next week." He told me that they had found the engine damaged and one wing tip crushed but wouldn't have to survey much, since the salt water hadn't had time to do permanent corroding.

The *Mary Ann*, in case you haven't heard of that famous lady, is a slow-chugging, flat-topped, rescue boat that operates around a naval air station. It chug-chugs out to the wrecked or sinking plane, swings its long-fingered crane hoist over one side, and lifts the unfortunate aircraft up by its tail onto the deck. The *Mary Ann* is the standard name for the salvage boats of this type in the Navy, and it is always great fun to bet whether she will get to the sinking aircraft.

If you stayed around and watched the procedure in this fuselage and wing shop, you would see the airplane stripped of all instruments, fabric, and detachable equipment. Then a spraying process would clean and prevent corrosion; paint, new fabric, and dope would complete the job. The overhauled engine, complete with instruments, comes in and is installed, the rigging crew checks alignment, inspection passes the completed overhaul, and the plane is pushed out for Mr. Pilot to fly—or bathe in the briny ocean again, depending on his luck. I moved down the floor, pausing to glance at a scout

AIR BASE

bomber, its wings drooping and wrinkled from a minor crash. It looked forlorn. This was where our worn-out or damaged airplanes would end up. I checked the list and went up to the next building, where parachutes are aired, inspected, and repacked monthly. (Incidentally, you don't have to jump in a parachute when you take on the job of earning your wings for Uncle Sam. And that's sensible. Why practice something you have to do perfectly the first time!)

The parachute packer lowered one of the billowy white chutes from its loft, pulled it taut across a smooth, clean table, and began to fold it. I had the urge to boast that I could do that, too, that we all had to learn it in Pensacola, but I didn't. And a good thing. The packer didn't make a wrong move or lose a motion. Within five minutes the chute was in its harness and ready for use. If I ever had any qualms about using a parachute, I have none now. That man, as were those around him, was as skilled a craftsman at an art as I have ever seen.

I had to hurry to get lunch at the ship service store. At this place, similar to the canteen of the Army, you can get meals, haircuts, have trousers pressed, shoes repaired, see the latest movies, and even stop at a post office to mail a letter off to the folks. It is a wonderful institution. You can buy anything from an ivory toothbrush to a Frigidaire here, less the discount. If they don't have it "Freddy" will get it for you "right away, sir, right away."

After lunch I walked down to the patrol-boat beach, where for blocks along the concrete ramp I watched launching and beaching operations going on constantly. I remembered, too, how at Pensacola we used to like to fly these air battleships around and put them through their paces. Their performance is stately and methodical, compared to the single-seat fighters and bombers, which are all action. These metal giants operate from San Diego Bay to form a scouting line hundreds of miles at sea, extending almost along the entire West Coast. Or they can set out on formation flights to Seattle, Hawaii, or the Canal Zone. I thought to myself, the hydroplane has come a long way since Glenn Curtiss lifted his crude pontoon clear of the waters of Spanish Bight.

Inside the hangars, right on the water ramp, several of the big flying boats were being overhauled and checked by scores of mechanics. They had to start early to get all the squadron planes in top condition for the big cruise and still continue flying daily schedules of bombing, gunnery, or scouting. On the cruise these planes would become the living quarters for ten or twelve men for days on end.

I started back for the squadron, watching the sections of snub-nosed Grumman fighters and a squadron of torpedo planes come whistling in over the edge of the field to roll their wheels along the big landing mat, seconds apart. Across the island you could see more and more sections, with now and then a single plane swinging around the edge of Coronado, parallel to the bight, crossing low over the bridge and sentries' gate to turn in and land just beyond the balloon hangar.

I have never grown tired of watching the squadrons coming home after a long day of flying. Even though I have done the same hundreds of times and have flown thousands of hours, there is something fascinating, something that holds your eye and thoughts, when an airplane lands. Go out to one of the big airports around the country—any day. If the weather isn't so foggy that even the sea gulls are "on instruments," you will find a crowd of people intently observing, straining and stretching to see airplanes come down out of the sky to get earth-borne again—even today, with airplanes as common as ships on the sea.

Back at the hangar I found the squadron had secured. Lieutenant Nuessle was still there going over some trouble reports.

"See everything on the station?" he asked. I told him I had the general picture.

"Well, next week we finish bombing and start carrier-landing practice on the field. We're due to go aboard the carrier for familiarization of new pilots in three weeks, when the *Lexington* comes down from Bremerton. With the big cruise close at hand we have to get everything in top shape as we go. You can act as liaison man between the shops here at the hangar and the supply depots on the station. We'll have four planes to turn in and replace with spares and six engines for overhaul. O.K?"

I learned to have a lot of respect for Nuessle— "Noz," as we called him. He was typical of the efficient junior lieutenants who have been trained for years to believe that "a job to do is a job to do well." As I started out he stopped me.

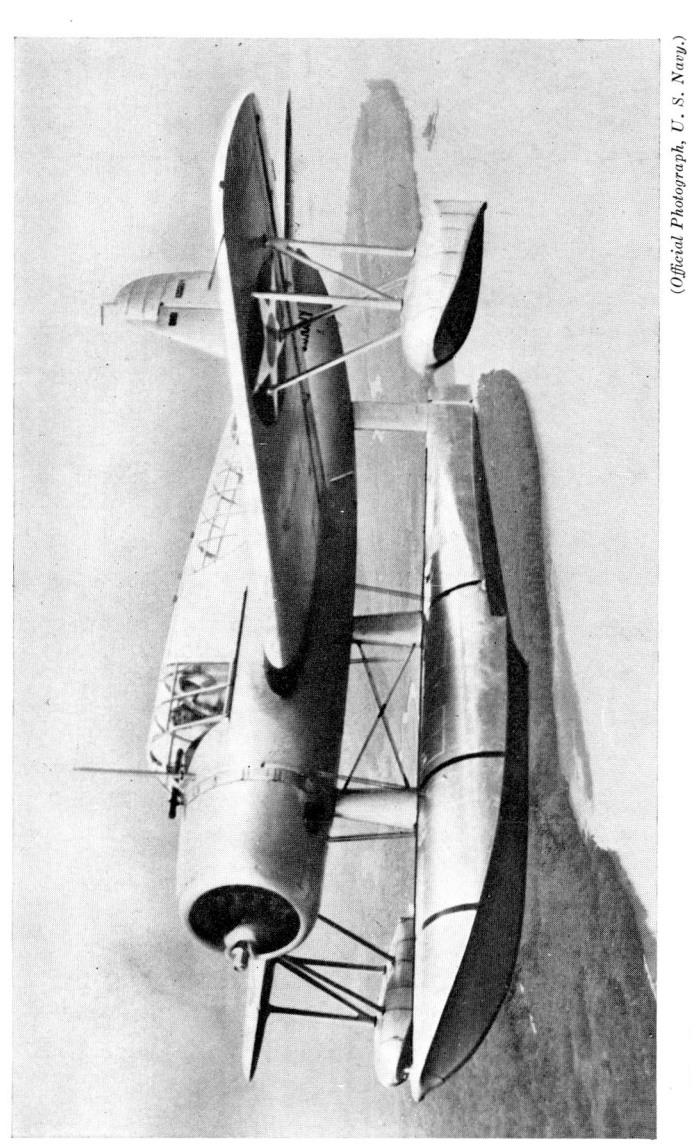

(Official Photograph, U. S. Navy.)

The hydro-airplane has come a long way since Glenn Curtiss lifted his crude pontoon clear of the waters of Spanish Bight.

"I forgot to tell you, Guy. The skipper is going to be at home this afternoon if you would like to make a duty call." I went home and changed clothes, kicking myself for not having thought of it before. You're supposed to call on your commanding officer shortly after reporting in the squadron. Usually you get the news as to when he will be at home, so that he somewhat expects company. That evening I paid my respects to Captain Alexander.

This business of making "duty" calls on commanding and executive officers when you are aboard an air station means in other terms calling on your friends. The custom has come down through the years. In the closely knit life that is centered around a service group, more or less apart from the society of the everyday world, there is need to know the men you work with. Naturally, it is customary for the junior officer to call on his senior.

When I sat down to talk to the captain (for the conventional fifteen minutes) he put me at ease immediately. He had been flying for twenty years; his stories and experiences were broad and full. As one of the first instructors at Pensacola he had initiated instrument flying, but not as we now know it. "Instrument flying then was flying by an altimeter, turn-and-bank indicator, and air-speed meter. We didn't know what a radio beam was and thought we were doing great things if we flew a half hour without looking outside the cockpit." Once, as a member of a squadron, the skipper had landed with seventeen other planes right in the middle of the Pacific Ocean when they couldn't locate the carrier and fuel ran low. I had heard about this adventure back in Pensacola and was anxious to get the straight story.

"Well, the carrier had launched all planes at about ten in the morning. Our outfit, flying single-seat Boeings, got off the deck first to get up above the ship as the combat patrol. After the deck was cleared of planes, we received orders to intercept an 'enemy' patrol and bombing group that our long-range scouts had picked up, so we closed up the formation and headed out to sea. After an hour and a half, the skipper spotted the group we were after, and we milled around them for a while, radioing in that the enemy had been intercepted and shot down. Then we headed back for the ship.

"We all knew it was going to be close then. Our

fuel was running low, and there appeared just enough to get back and land aboard. But after flying for an hour back to where the carrier was supposed to be, we couldn't see anything but the whitecaps coming off the rollers below. The carrier radioed her position again, and we changed course but ran into a cloud bank and some pretty foul weather. About this time, Number Seventeen radioed the skipper that he had some five or ten minutes of fuel left, and Number Eight spoke up with the same dope.

"Naturally, we were all in about the same shape, so I was happy to hear the captain say, 'O.K., Fighting One, we'll land as close together as possible on the water. Remember to full-stall your plane, have your parachute off, and be ready to pull the flotation release.' The old skipper was a calm gent. He just radioed the carrier our present position as near as he could figure and then circled down and landed. We all took our turns and in less than five minutes were sitting on the water in a big group on the top wings of the planes."

Alex lighted a cigarette, shooed away one of his youngsters, who had shyly crept into the room, and left me with mouth open, waiting to hear the rest.

"We had one wisecracker in the squadron, a fellow much like Vensel. This ensign—name was McCracken—kept yelling across to his roommate to go down, dig up some worms, and he would catch the fish for supper. The situation wasn't humorous, but Mac did keep the laughs rolling. As soon as we landed everyone got his rubber life raft out and tied it alongside, to be ready when his plane sank. [Flotation bags are good for anywhere from fifteen minutes to several hours, depending on water conditions and damage inflicted during the landing.] Then, too, it was pretty cold. The wind was strong and threw cold spray over you as it came off the whitecaps.

"Well, to make a long story short, one of the plane-guard destroyers pulled up about an hour afterward, and we were pretty happy to get aboard. They were able to save about six of the eighteen planes, but the rest sank. The crew found some dry clothes and blankets, and we gathered around the coffeepot until the carrier pulled up. The captain told us later that there had been sixty miles of wind where we had been flying and that we had landed thirty-five miles short of the ship." Modern navigation instruments have, fortunately, helped to eliminate such errors.

When I left his little bungalow the fifteen-minute duty call had run over an hour, a pleasant, interesting hour, the kind you never get tired of spending. I was glad "Noz" had dropped the hint.

Life aboard an air station is like that. You make a lot of friends and wrap your interests with theirs. You eat, sleep, and fly airplanes day and night, and all the particulars that go with them. Then, when you start talking, you find yourself on the same subject, whether you are at a bar, on the beach, or eating lunch. It doesn't get boring, either. If a discussion starts about politics, it usually ends up with the idea that the Republicans filibuster with Pratt and Whitney Wasps and the Democrats debate with Wright Cyclones! Hangar flying as we knew it in Pensacola was the nightly confab on the day's fortunes or misfortunes and dealt with instructors, checks, new stages of training. That is amateur stuff to what a fleet pilot of a year or so can hand out. His hangar flying will date back to the war games off the Mexican coast last year, the Earhart search, flights to Honolulu, the French Frigate Shoals, up to Alaska or down to Panama.

Sitting around the officers' club or stretched out on the beach, the men usually sound like this:

"Remember when Stevens hit the barrier that rough day coming back from Honolulu? The stern was pitching forty feet, and when you looked down the deck was there, and then it wasn't. Not a piece of that airplane left to make matches with, and old 'Hard Luck Stevens' crawls out, grinning that big, dumb grin of his, saying, 'Nothing ever happens. What a life!' Even the admiral on the bridge turned away to laugh. That was Steve's third crack-up on the cruise, and he wasn't actually to blame for any of them." Then someone will get back to the present.

"Did you hear about Johnston today? Son of a gun got eighty-four hits in fixed gunnery. Must be using buckshot. I couldn't punch that many holes in a target with an ice pick!"

"Well, if that's what all the gossip was about on the air while I was trying to radio in my last bombing run, that outfit should bow in shame. They must lean on their microphone buttons!"

So it goes. Before you leave the base you know enough amusing, harrowing, and tragic incidents that took place from Sitka to Guam to make you a professional at this business of hangar flying. What's more, you don't have to make them up. Your stories are true. I've found these bull sessions are an important part of this flying game and that much value can be derived from listening to the predicaments, the "close shaves" and "might haves" of other pilots. Operating from a big flying field with hundreds of other airplanes means knowing about a lot of different things that could happen and do happen in the air about you. The more of these you know of in advance the fewer the surprises that are in store for you.

Chapter IV

IN THE four years we spent at North Island, on the cruises out to Honolulu and in warring around the Pacific from the decks of carriers, our class lost only four men. This wasn't exceptional as a safety record, but it was good. Our class had numbered nearly forty on graduation, and when you consider the chances for accidents with each of these men doing hard, rugged flying and split-second timing—well, one in ten seems just about average.

Probably the first and foremost cause of crashes in aviation anywhere is carelessness—a fact that is just as true in service flying as anywhere else. But a supplementary cause of fleet crack-ups is the grasp for excellence and precision. Every man is proud of his squadron and its record, whether he out and says it or not, and he will "do his damnedest" to keep that record high. If you consider the amount of formation flying, the combat maneuvering in which each pilot must place implicit trust in the next man—running to eighteen in the squadron—then the small losses attributable to a base operating hundreds of planes a day are almost negligible. Human error in judgment and structural failure (very rare) of planes are other factors the grim reaper goes by. Smitty was overeager in his search for excellence. He was the "first" of our "four."

It is always great fun to chide a brother pilot from another squadron about his bombing, gunnery, dogfighting, or formation work. We usually had our best opportunity at lunch time, when we all gathered in the mess hall, eight to a table, for a hasty meal. Smitty was a member of Bombing One, a squadron that was still flying some old Martin dive bombers, and he teased easily.

"Smith, you don't expect to get any hits today on the *Utah*, do you?" Bud said. "Not in those coaster wagons of yours, anyway. I'd think the fleet would save those relics for the Smithsonian Institution or give them to Adolf as aid for the English." It seemed to be Smith's day to be "in the frying pan," so we all joined in. " . . . and tell me, Smitty," Foulds added, "how long does it take you to dive from ten thousand feet? Ten minutes, maybe? Or does the battleship back up and wait for you?" (A ten thousand-foot dive is only a question of seconds.)

Smith just laughed.

"O.K., gents, but we've been coming pretty close on practice so far, and on record diving today I've got a feeling I'll bounce mine right down the stack."

We all went out and drove back to our squadrons.

That afternoon we had hardly got into the air for some formation practice when the radio cracked in my ears. "Crash, crash, crash." It was our distress call sounding a crack-up somewhere, and I sat watching Nuessle's head over the wing, waiting for the information that was bound to follow.

"One Baker Seven calling Saratoga base station —one of our planes just went in off the port bow of the battleship! I didn't see a chute open and am heading for the spot now." The voice was hurried and tense. "Looked like Number Seventeen."

Immediately the air was alive with calls.

"Squadron leader, Bombing One to One Baker Seven—proceed to the crash, and give a report. All other planes Bombing One return to the base immediately!"

Then the base station came back. "O.K., number Seven, I've notified the *Utah* that bombing operations have ceased and to proceed to the spot of the crash. What number did you say that was?"

"I believe it was Number Seventeen," a voice spoke up.

Alex led us in a wide, sweeping circle, gave us the signal to spread out until the crash was settled. I had a sad feeling in my middle. If that was Number Seventeen it was Smitty's plane—and this was no movie. I hoped that by some remote chance he had got out and that the man in Number Seven had just failed to see the chute, but I knew the answer to that before it circulated through my mind. Then Number Seven plane of Bombing One reported that he was over the crash spot, circling, and could find only a big oil slick, with no trace of the plane.

The *Utah* radioed she was standing by with a small boat over the side and would make a routine search for any wreckage. I kept hoping that just by chance Smith hadn't flown that plane on this hop, and yet I knew that wasn't a fair thing to hope for either. But here was a man we had lived with, flown with for more than a year, and only an hour ago teased about getting a hit today. The skipper signaled to close up, and we completed our practice. On the way back to the field Noz turned around and looked back at me and shook his head, as if to say, "Too bad." I nodded back a "yeah" and tried to be just normal about the whole thing, but I wasn't too successful.

We landed, and I walked over to Squadron One to get the story. The officers were all standing around in their ready room, just talking quietly and trying to figure out what went wrong. It was quite unlike the usual routine of chatter about a hop, rolling the dicebox for cokes, or the bluster of someone's long-winded story that usually greeted you on entering a squadron ready room. They all felt badly about it, naturally. You watch accidents happen in other squadrons and are sorry, and you hope that it won't happen in yours. But you know the chances.

It seemed that Smitty had pushed over in his dive and gone down at the ship steeper than usual.

He had hung onto the target just a little too long to get his sights steady, and when he went to pull out there wasn't enough room. The pilot of the plane behind him said it looked as if he had got about halfway out of the dive and then hit the water. I left without asking questions and went back to the squadron. Late that evening the bomb-scarred old battle wagon *Utah* pulled into the bay to report that she had been unable to find any piece of the wreckage or either member of the crew.

The next afternoon we put on our dress uniforms and swords and attended the services in the little chapel next to the administration building, while Bombing One flew a formation parade over the water to drop flowers as a tribute to their two lost shipmates, Ensign Maynard Smith, and Radioman First Class, Edward Gentry. No undue sentiment, no downheartedness. It was just one of those things that happen every so often. The chaplain did a good job. His dissertation wasn't too long, and somewhere in the course of his eulogy came the old verse I've liked since our coach used to preach it before a college game.

>   —When the great Scorer comes to write
>   against your name,
>   He writes, not that you won or lost,
>   But how you played the game.

We all knew about Smitty, and we knew what would be "written." That night we all gathered around the officer's lounge and took up a collection for flowers to send Mrs. Smith. Then life and flying went right on as usual. And that is the part of fleet operations, the necessary part of the game in which you are indoctrinated early.

In fact, by the time the second member of our class hit the mast of a destroyer as he was coming aboard the carrier and spun in to join Smith several weeks later, we found ourselves so hardened to the fact that we simply added the mishap to our routine day, felt sorry about the misfortune, regretting the loss of another classmate with less display of sentiment than before, and carried on as usual.

I can't help remembering the incident that occurred in France one day, while I was testing dive bombers for the French Navy. I had gone over to prepare, assemble, and fly these planes for a French squadron down in Brest. The squadron was off the small carrier *Béarn* (later anchored at Martinique, her decks full of American planes for France at the time of that nation's capitulation), and the officers of the squadron were hurrying to check out in their new planes for embarkation.

One of the French lieutenants had taken off in a hurry and left his preheater turned to "cold," and ice formed in the carburetor shortly after take-off. We saw the plane settle lower and lower until finally it struck the wind-swept waters of the channel to flip its tail up in the air in a cloud of spray and sink. We knew the answer to that one, too. A diver recovered the plane next day with the young officer still at the controls. That same afternoon I had dinner with the captain of his squadron, wondering throughout the meal whether to be sad and offer sympathy or to be cheerful and gay in an attempt to cheer him up. I soon found that all I needed to do was act natural.

"It is too bad." Captain Mesny shrugged with that peculiar French manner of looking doubtful and helpless at the same time. "It is one of those things to expect. Last year we lost six." The rest of the evening went off as planned. The next day little or nothing was said about the accident, and flying had continued in the usual rush.

When flight operations ceased at North Island for the day, there was a general scramble for the tennis courts and swimming pools and a general relaxation from roaring power plants, rattling machine guns, and concentrated formation flying. The main objective of a service pilot who wants to maintain his efficiency is to keep his health in the pink. We found that this was far from difficult in the mild climate of southern California. By four fifteen you could hear the shouts and splashes coming from the two swimming pools adjacent to the officers' club and officers' lounge on South Field. Our twelve tennis courts were always full, and because of the exclusiveness of the base the game was performed with a "minimum of drag"—very little clothing on the human "fuselage." When you saw an untanned person on the courts, in the pools, or along the ocean beach you knew immediately that he was a newcomer or had been sick for an awfully long time. It would prove a long, hard search to find a group of several thousand individuals at once whose health surpassed that of the complement of North Island.

For double insurance to Uncle Sam's aviators and technicians, the sick bay was always open, and the Navy Medical Corps made it a business of keeping watchful eyes on the physical condition of the entire station. They were proud of *their* work, too. Every six months you are put through a complete physical examination, portraying every part of your anatomy to critical eyes, looking through eye-test machines, watching your blood count raise the eyebrows of the "doc," hoping you have enough spinach under your belt to get by the Snyder examination.

"Let me look at those teeth again." The dentist gets his share of looking you over.

"Ah, yes, I believe we had better pull those two wisdom teeth today and have it over with. Having any record firing at the squadron this week?" The doc keeps one hand on your shoulder as if to restrain your impulse to say yes and scram out in a hurry.

"No, doctor." (Meekly put.)

"O.K. Relax. You'll be back flying in two days. I'll call your skipper now. What's your squadron?" Then he calls up, squares things with the "old man," and out come two concretely impacted molars. You really don't mind, though, and are very happy to think that someone is actually looking after your best interests like a mother.

Besides looking after each person on the base, the medical corps is always ready to grab kits, scramble out the door of the sick bay into a warmed-up "meat wagon," and rush out, siren screaming, into the field to patch up a victim. It is easy to see what a good job they do in physically policing the base. The sick bay is always virtually empty, except for the early-morning sick call, when colds, stubbed toes, and minor cuts or ailments are taken care of in short order. The general prudential rule for personnel aboard—both flying and ground crew—is always, "Don't work when you're sick." This admonition is followed aboard the station, and I have yet to see anyone, officer or enlisted man, take advantage of its priority. The rule is a standard anywhere in the Navy.

Another rule I soon learned about, one that is more a tax on your common sense than anything else, is, "Don't fly over a solid overcast!" Uncle Sam would just as soon let the instrument flying, unless absolutely necessary, be done by the air lines in their scheduled work. He is not interested

AIR BASE

in pushing you out of the field in foul weather with a fast, valuable fighting plane, touchy to handle on instruments, in order to put over a flight. And most service pilots are far too busy to go through the process of practicing for hours, flying a beam, making procedure turns and letdowns to the field. They keep their hand in, but their business nine-tenths of the time is taken up with operating in formation, practicing gunnery or bombing. I had the unpleasant experience of discovering this fact one day, shortly after turning back over March Field to return to the base, and I learned a lesson.

The stratus clouds, which had been evident when I took off an hour earlier, had now formed into a solid overcast, stretching from the Laguna Mountains up behind San Diego, out over the water, and fog went right down to the ground. The gray mist ran along in a ragged line past the Army's base at March Field below Riverside and west across the ocean. Right then I should have remembered the base rule, "Don't fly over a solid overcast," and landed at this field, which was still in the clear. I didn't. That false sense of security and overconfidence an aviator sometimes gets was rattling along my gray matter. Why not try what one of the boys had figured out? If there is an overcast at the station, fly out to sea for four or five miles where you are sure there are no mountains, let down slowly until you get contact with the water, and then turn around and fly in to the coast line, and so back to North Island. It sounded good—why not? I knew there wasn't much gas left, but there should be enough. I looked back at the new radioman in the rear seat. He was bent over, playing with the transmitter, trying to learn all he could on this flight. It was one of his first. I started out toward the sea over the top of the white blanket.

After fifteen minutes I checked the fuel supply at twenty gallons and began to think that maybe this wasn't so smart after all. There was barely enough to return to the coast now. I felt sure that we were far enough out to let down, so down through we went, circling slowly, until at six hundred feet the water was visible below, though still through something of a mist. The fuel was getting lower, and I was feeling more and more uncomfortable, like the schoolboy who waits for the principal to cut the birch rod.

Then out of nowhere came what I thought at the time was the coast line—and I knew something was wrong. We had flown out to sea for fifteen minutes and back for only five before we had contacted land, and that couldn't be the mainland! As I flew along the edge of the rugged-looking brown cliffs and matted brush I got a sinking feeling right in the middle of my stomach. This just wasn't the coast line of those United States of America, or else it had changed in the past day! Turning north, I flew parallel along the edge of this unannounced piece of land and noticed that the fog level was below the top of the hills. Almost immediately we ran out of land to the north and had to turn east to stay in contact with shore line.

My heart sank, even before the squatty rows of houses appeared, stretching up the side of the mountain, and I knew where I had ended up. This was San Clemente Island—*sixty miles* out in the Pacific Ocean from the California coast line, and I knew we were in for it. The gas gauge was bouncing against the ten-gallon danger mark, and it was just a matter of minutes before we had to land.

The radioman in the rear seat spoke up through the interphones. "There is a field on top of the mountain, sir, if you have to land here. It's on the south end of the island."

I swung around, headed up the slope to the south, and ran smack into the fog before reaching the field. My heart sank like the fuel supply. That landing was out. The island was some eight hundred feet high, and the cloud bank was down to six hundred, entirely covering the field from sight. May as well face it, I thought. Here is your first crack-up, your first "boner," and you'd better hurry up. The gas was just about running out.

"Pull your belt up tight, Roberts, and brace your hands on the gun ring. I'll have to land in the water alongside the Marine pier back by the barracks. The field is in the fog.

"Aye, aye, sir. All set," Roberts came back quickly. He sounded nervous, and I couldn't blame him.

Then I saw it. Just a patch of open field running up the side of the mountain across a winding road that led down to the long rambling mess hall. Well, why not? If luck was with us we could save the plane, too, and after all—somebody must have landed on the side of a mountain before! Judging the angle of the slope, I figured out a carrier approach, dropped the wheels and flaps, and swung around up the side of the mountain. As the wheels rubbed I cut the gun, pulled back on the stick, and stood on the brakes. The effect was amazing. We didn't roll thirty feet, missed two boulders, bouncing over a third, and stopped short. I cut the switches, drew a deep breath, and jumped out on good, solid land. The plane didn't roll back, because one blown tire was resting against the rock that had cut it. That was the only damage.

"God, Mr. Guyton, that was swell—boy, that was swell," Roberts gave out as he slid down the side of the fuselage.

Then he looked kind of funny and blank, got just a shade white around the gills, and slumped down on the ground in as pretty a faint as a Victorian drawing-room madonna. I felt a little sorry for Roberts. After all, it had been his first flight with the squadron and one of his first in any airplane. He was just a youngster. When trouble comes, all a radioman or mechanic can do is sit back there and take it, not knowing whether you, the pilot, have everything under control or not.

That night I spent with the Marine contingent of San Clemente Island, having a drink on Ed and one on Al, everyone eager to entertain a visitor from the base who "got away with murder." Then the next day we hooked up the rattling tractor to the plane, towed it up to the field, and scampered back to North Island. As I walked into the office Alex met me.

"Well, glad to see you are back safe. We got your message O.K. last night from the Marine base at San Clemente. How in the world did you happen to end up over there?"

I told him that everything looked just rosy for a letdown through the overcast out to sea and that then I had planned to fly back east to the field.

"Of course, you know," Alex said, "I'll have to put you under 'hack' [the customary first offender's discipline in the Navy] for about ten days. I'm sorry, Guyton, but the last orders from the commandant were to discipline everyone who broke a regulation. That one has been strict for eleven years now, as I remember it."

I knew that the skipper didn't like to hand out the discipline any more than I liked the idea of not being able to fly for ten days, but in my heart I knew he was perfectly right. My mistake, my stupidity hadn't cost a life, hadn't cost Uncle Sam anything, but look what could have happened! I nodded that I understood and went out to tell the flight officer to hold me off of the schedule for the next ten days. I had learned my lesson.

That night, of course, Bud had a great time rubbing it in. "Oh, so you want to fly some cross-ocean hops, huh? So you like the marines after all? Aren't you just a little bit ashamed of all the names you have called us now? Suppose there hadn't been anything on San Clemente but mountain goats or sea gulls? I'll have more respect from you in the future, Ensign Guyton." And so it went for the next week.

And for ten days I reported at the squadron to stand the duty-officer watch, write the aircraft-trouble reports, fill out the logbooks, and play general handyman until my "sentence" was served. When the squadron went out for their first day of fixed gunnery I felt very much like the first-string fullback who was benched until he learned his signals better. But—I had learned my lesson.

On the tenth day, Sperry Clark, signal officer of the *Lexington*, the man who "brought you aboard," came into the squadron early in the morning.

"This list will report with their respective planes that they will operate on the cruise to Border Field tomorrow morning for carrier-landing practice:

Fields, Stuart, Ewers, Smith, and Guyton. Keep in formation until you see the yellow flag on the field. Then break up, and space yourselves in the groove. You will get ten or twenty landings on the field, and if everything is O.K., we'll send you out to the ship Saturday morning for your final check-out. And remember, you birds"—Sperry was intimate with every man he brought aboard the carrier, and he had a hundred pilots to take under his wing for the cruise—"obey the signals, and use your heads,"

We nodded, a little thrilled about it all, and Sperry went out. The smell of the big cruise was in the air. It was just three weeks off.

Chapter V

JUST what I had expected to find on initial contact with the social end of the United States Navy I am not sure. Back in Pensacola we had not even come close to understanding the "because" of this small world in itself, all wrapped up with tradition, custom, and convention. In Pensacola we simply get a round robin of teas, maybe a cocktail party, and a lot of officers'-club dancing in between.

Actually, we weren't down there to attend pink teas with the commandant's daughter, and the commandant's daughter usually knew it. She was wary, to say the least, of cadets in training and generally had a date with the instructor when we called. It didn't really bother us much, because after a full day of flying and then in addition a couple of nights a week infiltrated with ground school, navigation, and radio, we just couldn't get excited about the weaker sex for the yawns that went around.

We had learned very shortly back there in the blackjack and scrub oak that the kind of flying we had embarked on was work, not play. The bands didn't play, and the crowds didn't cheer when we came taxiing up to the line after several hours of bombing or formation practice. The only thing that met us was the officer in charge of flight operations, who would usually bring such glad tidings as, "Rifle drill at five thirty in front of the barracks." Or, "There will be a lecture tonight in the auditorium on discipline and leadership in the Navy. Everyone will attend." So went our weeks.

But now we found ourselves a part of the Navy, stripes and all, and, stripes and all, it was new to us. Bud came bouncing into the room one night with a silly grin on his big Boston mug and plopped down on the bunk, laughing.

"O.K., Mr. Martin," I said, "What's up?" I folded up the carrier-landing procedure I had been studying and shelved it. There was no use in trying to get any reading done with Basil in the near vicinity, especially if he had something to get off his chest.

"My good man," he said, slipping his shoes off and wrinkling his toes against the wall. (Bud was generally flat on his back when nothing was going on.) "We have just been invited to the commandant's reception, where all the little Navy and Marine Corps Juniors will hold forth in their finery to welcome the first class of young officers into the fashionable realm of Navy society. We are expected with our ladies, my boy, at the commandant's quarters on the base at five for cocktails tomorrow afternoon."

"What's so funny about that, junior?" I put in.

"Oh, so you don't get it," Bud said. "Young fellow, you are invited to your first social function of any note in the Navy, 'with your lady,' and you don't get it! Well, be so kind as to explain to this exalted marine just where in hell you will find your 'lady' of the evening."

I began to see the light. In the time we had been here there was so much going on in getting organized and familiar with things in general that we hadn't had the time to get around to the women.

"In other words," Bud went on with a big

stretch, "there will be many pretty young things there for you to meet, and you are going because the Navy Juniors want to make you feel at home and acquaint you with the relaxing side of this service life."

"Anyone else we know going?" I asked.

"Yep. Ewers, Foulds, Jensen, Hitchcock, practically everyone in our class. There is an invite in my pocket, and as soon as I wake up I'll give it to you." Bud was practically snoring.

Next day we had "Lotus Leaf," our Philippine mess attendant, take our dress blues down to the cleaners, and by the time five o'clock rolled around we were shining like a battle wagon's brightwork. Then we piled into "Hotdamn" and drove down past the armory to the palm-shaded, rambling stucco house that belonged to Admiral Gannon. It was set back from the field toward the bay, surrounded by palm trees and ferns. It was enough to make you rub your eyes when you thought that not a thousand yards away was the buzzing, bustling, flying field. I wondered how the admiral ever got any sleep when night flying was on, for I distinctly remembered how often planes landed on a one-ball course, just skimming those trees and that flat roof. You can't just ignore a thousand-horsepower Cyclone turning a propeller in low pitch—if it's right above you. Not unless you're stone deaf.

You may not appreciate what these social gatherings mean to the new and totally strange bachelor officer aboard an air base for the first time. I'm sure I didn't. But since the regulation had stated that "all men who want to join the Naval Air Corps as cadets must be single," this sort of function was the appropriate and well-founded method of introducing the new men. You will find that it is prevalent at any large air station or base, both Army and Navy, and quite unlike similarly performed functions "outside" the service. Men in the Navy, from flying officers to submarine officers, from battle-wagon crew to destroyer crew, all speak the same language. That is Navy and anything pertaining to the Navy.

They are so taken up with their branch of the service and its relation to the other branches that the world outside is actually moved into the background. They live, eat, and sleep their profession. I know of many officers, who, having spent a week at sea aboard a battleship, will remain aboard when the ship hits a port they have been to several times before. If the stop is only for a few hours or a couple of days, they are much more interested in a good book or a nice long session of bridge aboard a gently rolling and quiet home than they are in going ashore to raise a little particular hell. After several years on sea duty, such an attitude grows on you, and, oddly enough, it makes sense.

"Admiral Gannon, may I present Ensign Guyton, Lieutenant Martin, Ensign Foulds, Ensign Ewers. . . . " One of our commanding officers took us in hand.

We found the admiral a genuine personality, interested, like any senior officer, in our squadron and squadron commander and how we liked the service in the fleet so far. "Glad to have you aboard, gentlemen. I hope your tour of duty is a pleasant one and we can get better acquainted before long. You'll find cocktails on the table. Please make yourselves at home."

From out in the patio came the twang of Hawaiian music, well played. It was broken now and then by a late squadron plane roaring in overhead to whistle past the house and thump down on the field. We moved through the room, meeting more and more of the air-station officers and their wives and daughters. Wherever we paused in a group we found that talk, reminiscence, jokes were all made up of Navy and old shipmates. I believe that a Navy man has more friends, more widely scattered friends, than anyone else in the world.

"Who? old John Townsend! Say, I saw him last May down in Honolulu, when we pulled into Pearl Harbor for maneuvers. John is still executive officer of Patrol Squadron Six. And remember Charlie Bradley? Well . . ."

At first you feel just a bit like an outsider as the discussion of "old so-and-so" goes on, but it isn't but a short year or so before you find yourself in the thick of it. Service people change residences so often, because of change of duty, that it isn't long before "Ed" is down in Coco Solo, "Frank" over in Norfolk, "Bart" gone to the new base at Guam. It happens that way, and you are constantly running into old shipmates in any of the odd places in the world. When you meet them, at once "that time in Tijuana at the Foreign Club" or "when Bill hit the stacks on the Saratoga coming aboard" will flash through your mind. Then you both sit down and rehash the last four or five years, letting your hair down and barring no holds.

The most amazing and peculiar chance meeting like this I have run into was about a year after I had left the fleet. It occurred in Paris the night that war was declared on Germany. That night we had had our first alert. As I left my hotel room to stumble down the dark, trunk-cluttered hallway, I was swearing in the best American French I could muster. All day we had spent putting helpless people on trains in the big rush to get out of town. Americans were going home, to Spain, Portugal, Switzerland, anywhere away from blackouts and dreaded war bombing. I had captured at least three stray babies that day in overflowing railway stations and had tired a not too competent brain with hard-thought French sentences. Now, about midnight, just after the city had gone to sleep, came the moaning and wailing of the siren, followed by a rapping on the door. *"L'abri, monsieur, l'abri, s'il vous plaît!"*

Across the hall I heard some honest-to-goodness swearing that was typical Southern United States style and a dead giveaway for the swamps of Georgia. There was such a scramble in the blackness, however, that I just picked my way along behind the crowd. Then, as I had rounded the last flight of stairs and come out into the lighted wine cellar, someone let out a yowl that made the more reserved peer down their excited noses.

"Guy, you god-damned dive-bombin' Yankee fool, what are you doin' heah?"

"Larry Seymour," I shouted as I saw him struggling through the crowd. Then we wrapped up in a good Navy free-for-all until the proprietor, mindful of his wine stock, stopped us.

I'll never forget that night. Larry had been in the second class at Pensacola, had been sent out to a cruiser for duty, and I hadn't seen him for three and a half years. Back in training, we used to spend half of our free evenings in the barracks imposing on his good nature by teasing him about his Southern drawl or refighting the Civil War in his bunk. Imagine running into him in a cold, damp, Paris bomb cellar with a war going on! I couldn't get over it. We uncorked a bottle of wine and went over the past years, day for day. He had just pulled into Paris that night from Le Havre, having been sent over as test pilot for another company.

And that is just how it happens. If you have ever run into someone in a strange out-of-the-way spot, someone you have eaten with, flown with, seen eye to eye with years ago, you will know what I mean. It's a great reunion.

When we left the commandant's party we had met sixty or seventy people we would see off and on for the next couple of years, had been invited to several more parties, down at the beach, over at the club, and with so-and-so's squadron. Our week ends would be full until the cruise left for Honolulu, and we were no longer strangers in a new environment.

As we stepped outside into the twilight the roar of night flying filled our ears. Fighting Three was making night-carrier approaches at the field, and every few minutes a pair of flaming exhausts and red and green running lights would rumble across the tops of the trees to settle against the black apron of the field.

"Let's drive out to the edge of the mat and watch how the boys are making out," Bud said. We dimmed the lights and pulled up at the edge of the big balloon hangar, where we could see the green lighted wands wave the planes in as they came down the groove. The "groove," incidentally, is a much-used term around an air base. Actually, it is an imaginary air space behind the stern of an aircraft carrier. When the pilot turns his plane into the groove he is prepared for a landing. From that point on until the plane hits the deck he watches and follows the signals from the signal officer standing on the stern of the carrier. In practicing landings on the field, it is understood that the same straight line of imaginary air space lies directly behind the markers that replace the carrier deck. Sperry Clark, who stood out in the inky blackness signaling with those wands, had one of the toughest jobs in the whole air detachment—I would almost say in the whole of naval aviation, but that might give rise to some dispute. Just the same, I have yet to see a particular job that can and does actually make a man prematurely gray-haired as fast as this job of signaling airplanes aboard a carrier.

Even as we watched, the lighted wands went up to make the landing signal, dipped when the approaching plane was getting too low, and came back to the original signal as the pilot brought his plane back to the proper altitude. As the plane roared across the edge of the mat, hanging on the gun, the pilot got the familiar "cut," meaning "cut your gun," as Sperry drew one of his wands across his throat. The fat-bellied little Grumman hovered for an instant, just a bulky black shadow from where we sat, and then squatted down on the tar with a crunch. A blast of throttle, and he was back in the air in a turning climb, his red and green wing lights cutting a strange arc across the sky.

I began to realize the responsibility that rests on the signal officer. He must know immediately, standing on the edge of a carrier deck, when a plane is too fast or too slow, when it is too low or too high, and, more than that, he must anticipate the move of the individual pilot. Many a time during a cruise I have gone back to the signal platform on the stern of the *Lexington* to watch the planes being brought aboard. Sitting down low on the sternmost ladder, you could hear Sperry waving his signals and talking to himself as a pilot overcontrolled coming down the groove. "All right, Jackson, get your nose up, get your nose up. Damn it all, you can see this signal, Jack, old boy, get it up, get it up."

Looking out across the white wake of the carrier some forty or fifty feet below to the approaching plane as it turns in ahead of the plane-guard destroyers is an education in itself. Then to realize that the man with the two paddles behind you is signaling that plane across the chasm that separates its wheels from the churning ocean below makes you begin to wonder. But not for long. You find yourself in the plane the next flight, peering out of the cockpit at old Sperry and trying your damnedest to make a good approach for him. A signal officer is appointed, among other reasons, for his ability to understand a man and to get that man to *want* to put out his best.

But flying aboard a carrier for the first time is designed to be one of the choicer moments in your flying career. Hundreds have done it before and done it many times. Hundreds will do it again. Yet that first trip up the groove, that first "cut" signal behind the narrow pitching and rolling deck, is still the ace of them all. Your wheels are over water, then over deck, and then you find yourself holding onto the throttle, just a bit breathless as you wait for the arresting gear to stop all forward motion suddenly.

The pilot generally forgets all the little reminders like, "Taxi fast as soon as you get free of the gear. Don't sit there after you land. Get going so the next plane can land aboard." He is usually too much pleased with his success at actually getting safely aboard and is a bit flustered at first. This attitude changes after the first couple of landings. But that is one of the reasons why the new pilots are trained first to hit an imaginary deck marked off on some outlying field, away from the base, before going out over the ocean to land aboard. On land the signal officer works for several days, if necessary, to make sure that the pilot knows how to follow signals and what to do in case he gets in a jam coming up the groove. And it is mandatory that you place implicit trust in the signal officer. The inevitable happens when you don't.

Next morning the five of us climbed into our planes and took off for Border Field. As we circled southward, out past Point Loma toward Mexico, Stuart, who was leading, signaled for right echelon, and we slid over into position, ready for the breakup. As we swung over the field I could see Sperry setting up his red flags to mark off the carrier deck, his little "sky taxi," a Consolidated Trainer, pushed off to one side under a cluster of trees. Then the yellow flag went up at one end of the platform. Bill waggled his wings, rolled away from the formation, and started the circle. We spaced ourselves, lowered our landing gear, and followed each other around to get in the groove. Then, one by one, we swung in and headed for the "deck," watching Sperry's signals.

Too high, too high, now too low. A little fast, just a little. Take off some gun. Put in on, you're sinking! Now—there is the R signal, and I'm doing O.K. Get the nose up, he says. There— cut! I flashed past Sperry and hit the dirt between the rows of flags but was far too close to one edge. That is how *not* to make carrier landings on a deck if you don't want to go over the side. Now put on the throttle, and climb out of the field in a turn. Watch the man ahead, and don't get too close or you'll buck his slip stream all the way in. Some game!

After about an hour Sperry beat his paddles on the ground to signal us to land. We did and listened to our lecture.

"Look, you fellows," he said, after the last man had climbed out of his plane and slipped off his parachute. "You can't come down the groove at ninety knots and expect to land on the deck! Not unless the carrier has grown since I was aboard last.

Remember, when I give you the slow-down signal you've got to slow down, haul your nose up a little without climbing, and then keep it that way. You, Ewers, you keep edging over toward the right-hand side of the platform. Get squared away sooner, and fly straight up the groove, or you'll end up against the stacks with a shirt full of bones! And you, Guyton. When I signal you a high dip it doesn't mean to bury the airplane in the weeds. Just ease it down a shade lower, and then hold it there." From head to foot Sperry was covered with dust, blown back on him as the planes hit and blasted the dirt back when they took off again.

"O.K. Let's try it again. Try to follow the signals a little closer, and you'll all do all right."

We climbed back into the planes, their engines still turning over at the edge of the field, and one by one took off to get into the landing circle. Then around and around we would go for more practice at "bouncer drill," as we nicknamed this field warm-up. It didn't take long to find out that real finesse was called for to fly down the straight and narrow path toward the signal officer, keeping just the right speed and just the right altitude. Flying low and slow in aviation is still the point at which mistakes cannot be made—if good health is to be preserved. This kind of flying was just about as low and as slow as the airplane could be flown, but it was interesting work and an opportunity for the pilot to show his skill.

For another hour we went at it, circling and bouncing, flying by signals, cutting the gun, bouncing, always trying to make the next one "just right." Then Sperry waved us home. We joined up over the ocean off the beach, let down into the landing lane that followed the Silver Strand up the bay, and swung around over Spanish Bight to land at North Island. Sperry came in a few minutes later to join us in a coke around the squadron table and give us the news. He said that we had all done pretty fair at the last and that we were to be ready to qualify aboard the carrier when she came down from Bremerton in a few days.

"Well, they had better get out the crash kit and the stretchers," Nuessle said, propping his feet up on a chair. "New blood. Yes, sir, more new blood."

"Oh, come on, Noz," Kane put in with a wink. "You know carrier landings aren't as hard as that. Why the last three new bloods to qualify only got busted heads and lost a few teeth. Of course, I admit, Stephens, you did a better job. But who wouldn't when a wheel flys off as you hit the deck!"

The boys had their little jokes, and to help them out we just grimaced and acted a little more nervous about going aboard. As a matter of fact, we did begin to think there was more to this carrier operation than the way it sounded when you said, "Land aboard."

Chapter VI

THERE is a certain spirit of camaraderie in the service everywhere. Loyalty runs up as well as down. Enlisted men will give their right arm at any time to help an officer of any rank or station, and the officer will hang on until the last ditch to aid the men he commands. This loyalty is not the sentimental mush you find in stories or articles or a glamorous impetus to the interest of a hero-worshiping people such as Americans like to be. It is not talked, discussed, or advertised at any base or aboard any ship or station. Still, I have yet to see the time when one shipmate in the Navy wouldn't go through hell and high water in his unassuming but determined way to save the face or lives of the crew around him. It's just an unwritten law. One such incident, though it proved futile, occurred as all units prepared for embarkation on the big cruise not two weeks off.

Each squadron was now busy equipping fully, repairing, and obtaining new material to have all eighteen planes in readiness for shoving off aboard the carriers. The heads of all departments, flight, engineering, radio and communications, navigation, and gunnery, were busy as worker bees checking over their supplies and putting all gear in top shape. Nuessle and I scurried back and forth between the squadron hangar and the supply station, obtaining spare wings, engine replacements, wheels, instruments. We ran Lyons, the line chief, into a state of nervous anticipation every time we approached him.

"How about Number Seven, chief?" "Has it been checked yet?" "Did you test the flotation gear in Fourteen and Eighteen?" "Lyons, we've got to give engine checks to the second division from Nine to Nineteen immediately after qualification landings aboard the carrier tomorrow. That means checking the planes at night, so have a section on duty when working hours are over from now on."

Lyons would just make little notes in his black book, scratch his wiry head, and calculate. "Aye, aye, sir," he'd always answer and then by some persuasive power, or his adequate knowledge of how to get the most out of his men, would have the jobs completed on time.

There is an old saying that the chiefs—the chief petty officers—run the fleet. They are like the top sergeants in the Army. It isn't far wrong. They have come up the ranks from apprentice seamen and have ten to thirty years of rugged duty behind them, and they know about all one human being can know about Uncle Sam's fleet. You will have the utmost respect for the chiefs as they show you how to handle a boat crew, tell you what to watch out for on the quarter-deck, explain various and sundry parts of the Navy that you, as a tenderfoot, have yet to encounter.

Such a man was Lyons. With never a hint as to his superior knowledge, he would gladly take an hour of his "behind-schedule time" to show you just what happened to Two Baker Six when the engine burned out and why it occurred. You learn to profit by his explanations, and they are invaluable. Then, when he is all finished, he will end up with something like, "Are you all squared away now, sir?" And you actually tingle with the loyalty portrayed by a man whose heart is big, whose job is hard, and whose experience of years, coupled with the knocks of a long road, is so generously given.

One afternoon, in the midst of the hum of preparation, the skipper came out of his office with a dispatch in his hand. He called the duty officer to round up all the officers and then sat down at one end of the long green table. Outside we had planes and equipment scattered all over the front apron of the hangar. Life rafts were being stowed, cowling replaced, machine guns installed. Here and there an engine was being turned up while a mechanic went over his check sheet. The painter was busy brightening up the wings and insignias.

"A dispatch just came down from the commandant," Alex said when we were all seated around the ready room.

"Commander Hawley, flying an air-station plane, is lost somewhere between San Diego and Palm Springs. He gave his departure report from Palm Springs six hours ago and is four hours overdue now. Weather up at operations said that there was a low ceiling over the mountains at the time and that the clouds were down below the high peaks up around the Palomar. The commandant has designated searching areas for four respective squadrons to begin a search immediately." Alex let that soak in and then went on.

"Our area for the search will be the sector from San Diego east across the Laguna Mountains to Imperial Desert, north just beyond the observatory on Palomar Mountain, and due west to the flat slope at Oceanside. How many planes do we have available for immediate flight, McClure?"

Mac, the flight officer, ran over his list. "The first division is intact, captain, but the rest of the planes are still in check. They can be available tomorrow morning if we work straight through tonight."

There was hardly a sound in the ready room as we tried to picture where Hawley might have crashed and why. I could see the jagged peaks running their rocky slopes up to eight, nine thousand feet in that territory, and I knew what a search would mean in that pine-covered, rugged country. We would have to fly right down over the treetops, climb up and down the sides of the mountains, aim for passes, if a crashed plane was to be located in that sector.

"All right," the skipper said. "The first division will man planes immediately and take off to begin the search. Spread out when you get up there, and each man take his part and pick it clean. Keep your fuel on reserve tank all the time, and don't forget that a forced landing will mean cracking up in some pretty nasty country. You'll have to look sharp. That small plane wouldn't leave much of a mark where it went in."

We all got our maps, marked off sections for each man, and climbed into flight gear. As we were going out the door to man planes, the captain issued a final order. "Stay up two hours, and then return to the base. The second team of nine will be ready to take off immediately after the planes are regassed. We'll fly until dark."

The nine of us trotted out to the line, climbed into the warmed-up planes, and took off by sections, rendezvousing over Point Loma and heading northeast. Three other squadrons, Scouting Two, Bombing Three, and the "hot shots" of Fighting Two, roared out after us to take up their search. As we neared the big silver dome that poked out of the Palomar Mountain top, Stuart, who was leading, swung wide to escape a formation of fighters escorting a tow plane home. They had been off in their area practicing gunnery runs on the target the tow plane was hauling along behind it. Obviously they hadn't heard of the lost plane, for they were close to the designated area and would have broken up their gunnery practice to lend a hand immediately.

We broke up, and each plane headed for the spot the pilot had marked off on his map. The low scud-cloud formations were almost disseminated, and the ceiling now was well above the highest peak. Up north, behind Los Angeles and above Riverside, I could make out the prodding snow-capped tip of Mount Gorgonio, some thirteen thousand feet above sea level. Then I ducked down low over the treetops and began to strain for some sign of the lost plane.

I had visions of spotting a black, charred mass against the side of some rocky peak and radioing in, "Just spotted crash—directions following." Or of seeing a tangled silver fuselage crumpled in one of the many passes that sliced the rocky terrain, with a lone figure beside it waving. These were the visions of a would-be rescuer. I couldn't help feeling a little lump in my throat as I imagined what any plane that had to go down in this godforsaken waste would look like. I have seen what comes out of a crushed cockpit when a plane hits the earth at several hundred miles an hour, and I have no desire to see it again. It is not pretty to look at, especially if the remnants of the human being in the cockpit has bought you your nightcap at the lounge the evening before.

By the end of the first hour I could tell that it was going to be more than difficult to find that plane if it had landed in this part of the woods. I flew up and down the side of the mountain, not fifty feet above the treetops, jumping high ridges, diving into gullies, peering down between the slender pine trunks, trying to catch a glimpse of what might have been a plane. Nothing. I tried to think what Hawley's route would have been, how the prevailing wind might have drifted him, and, then, where he might possibly have gone in under those circumstances. Then I'd get to the spot, circle and circle the obvious points of initial contact with the ground under those circumstances, and find nothing but gray stones, broken tree trunks staring back at me. You must be around here somewhere, commander, but where, where?

At the end of two hours the radio cracked in my

ears startlingly, and Stuart's somewhat tired voice came through the earphones. "Bombing Two planes, rendezvous on me at four thousand over the observatory."

We joined up a few minutes later, the other eight planes appearing from all angles to skid up into their respective positions. Then we returned to North Island. On the way back Kane, flying the other wing position in my section, looked across the empty space and slowly shook his head as if to say, "No soap." I nodded back an affirmative. Finding anything short of a pinnacled citadel in that man-forgotten country would be a tough job for Superman. Back at North Island the second nine pilots were ready and waiting for us. Lyons had all planes gassed in record time, and not twenty minutes after we had landed the second group rolled down the taxi line, formed into three plane V's out on the mat, and took off. They would be good until dark, so our chores for the day were over.

"We'll follow the same schedule for tomorrow morning," Mac said as we pulled off flight gear and discussed the possibilities of finding the lost plane. The other eight pilots had been up against the same kind of terrain in their respective territories and weren't too hopeful of the chances. Then we shoved off to get some rest and be ready to go at daybreak.

For four days this continued. All gunnery exercises, carrier work, and radio practice were called off in order to facilitate the search. (By the end of the fourth day I felt that I could get to sleep easier if I just kept my parachute strapped on my back!) There was not the slightest trace of the missing plane.

At the end of the fourth day of this strained, nerve-taxing flying a dispatch came down from Operations. "It is believed that further search is unnecessary and that Commander Hawley might have flown seaward and been forced down out in the ocean. Discontinue further operations."

Alex had never shown his feelings about anything before, but when we received this last dispatch, I noticed it. He simply told McClure to arrange the flight schedule for the next day as always and to have the qualification planes and pilots stand by to take off for the carrier at noon. But his eyes mirrored a reflection of the lost commander, for whom there was but one answer, and he seemed just a little more beaten down than he had ever appeared before. The whole four days of the trying search Alex had been in the thick of it, though as captain he might easily have carried on with his office work and left the flying to the rest of the squadron. It wasn't until several weeks after that I found out Hawley had been his classmate back in '18. So it goes sometimes. To this day there has been no trace of the missing plane and its lone occupant.

An air base or air station is a unit of the United States Navy that has a function somewhat of its own. In a sense it is in organization like a battleship, with its own commanding officer, staff officers, departments, and divisions working in complete coordination as a single unit. The main purpose of every air base is to support the national policies and interests of the United States, its continental and overseas possessions. That is its purpose in conjunction with the fundamental policy of the United States Navy. The direct function of an air base is the support of naval operations, and those naval operations stretch from the icy waters of the faraway Aleutian Islands to the tropical thunderstorms in Panama, from the bases at

Trinidad and Antigua to the rock-strewn coast of Nova Scotia.

In such a scheme you find North Island taking its place in a triangle of protection and defense that runs from Alaska to Hawaii to the Canal Zone. Long-range patrol bombers take off from the sheltered bay at San Diego to fly a constant patrol out nearly a thousand miles over the ocean, constantly on the alert for enemy submarines or—if war comes—enemy raiders. They report by radio, and the aircraft carriers, if they aren't already at sea, pick up their escort and shove off to perform the mission at hand. A marine detachment remains at the air base along with several squadrons of fighters and bombers, ready for an emergency of the moment.

When carriers, patrol planes, and destroyers return, the base furnishes an undiminishing supply of fresh stores, equipment, spare parts, and quick overhaul for the units that require repairs. Then back out to sea goes the fleet air arm to protect the long coastal shore line and the surrounding waters in the vicinity of Lower California. Also, the base at North Island, with its outlying fields, meets the requirement of extensive flight training and practice that is so vital to the aviator flying in the Navy to keep in fighting form with a "well-versed gunnin' eye." In fact, you soon find that an air base is a place that really hums with activity and excitement, especially when the country is in a state of national emergency and when every pilot, plane, and squadron has to be in top shape every minute of every hour!

After you have become accustomed to the routine, the duties, the people, and the surroundings, life aboard an air base settles down, for the most part, comparable to a businessman's eight-hour day. Oh, you have several duties and watches to stand at odd hours during the week, and with the national emergency on your days stretch out somewhat, but all in all, aboard the base, you find time to enjoy life in a pretty normal fashion. You bounce out at seven, scramble over to breakfast at the officers' mess, and then reach the squadron by eight. Usually there will be three or four flights scheduled on the board, and you find that you have to hustle to get in a half hour of radio-code practice before taking off on the first of these flights. Then out to the designated squadron area you go to unleash the rattling machine guns at a target sleeve or to pull the bomb releases for a potential bull's-eye on the dive-bombing target. You may be dogfighting with another squadron, in which case it is necessary to rendezvous with them by prearrangement before attempting to "shoot 'em down." When five o'clock comes around you begin to wonder where the day went. Flying strain catches up with you later—usually after you've had a nice big dinner. If it's your turn on the security watch—and it will be once or twice a month—the remainder of the evening is still Uncle Sam's.

A security watch, stood in four-hour shifts, represents somewhat the job of police chief. Each squadron hangar, office building, armory, and the immediate surrounding grounds are policed throughout the night by a sentry. As the day closes the sentry takes up his flashlight, web belt, and gun and begins his rounds of inspection. The security watch officer takes his post in the "shack," ready to answer the phone in case of emergency, making his rounds periodically to see that a sentry who may have had a hard night before isn't dozing.

As I assumed the watch one evening I decided to hunt up a sentry who had made lots of carrier landings aboard a carrier and learn what I could

—off the record—in order to be competently primed for tomorrow. The stars twinkled through a perfect Southern evening as I walked along the edge of the field beyond the rows of hangars lining West Beach. It is almost unbelievable how quiet and peaceful an air station can get at night when flying stops. After a day full of roaring engines, clattering machine guns, or droning formations, the still night is like a summer evening in the Ozarks back in Missouri. The reaction is even stronger when you gaze around the dull, lighted hangars, far around to South Field, knowing what potential dynamite is stored in each and how bustling will be the spot you're standing on tomorrow morning. For a few minutes I watched the rotating beacon atop the balloon hangar flash white and green through the night into the sky. A beacon is an angel's eye to an aviator. Its constant vigil goes on through the night as though beckoning a wanderer. Then I walked over to Fighting Two's hangar.

"Evenin', sir." The sentry snapped out a salute with his salutation. I saw at once that he was a chief naval aviation pilot, one of the well-known Fighting Two "Hotshots." A squadron of enlisted men, led by officers, they are known as the best bunch of fliers in the fleet.

"Good evening, sentry," I said. "Everything O.K.?"

"Yes, sir. Just checked the armory, locked up the gas truck, and put on a fresh pot of Joe. Will you have some, sir? It's probably percolated enough."

We went in to the coffee mess, found some cups, and poured ourselves some of the fresh-smelling coffee. "Chief," I asked, trying not to appear too much the novice, "how much of a jolt is it when you stop after hitting the deck aboard the carrier? I understand it isn't so bad, but suppose the deck is pitching."

The chief took out a worn-looking pipe, knocked the bowl against a machine-gun butt, and filled it. "Well, that depends a lot on how you get aboard," he said. "If you're fast when you get the cut, chances are you'll pull up pretty short. Not so as to jar you too much. It will just force you up against the belt and hold you there for a couple of seconds —maybe massage your breadbasket a little. Of course, if the stern is coming up when the signal officer gives his cut, you want to be careful not to push the nose over too far. It'll slap you down pretty hard."

I could already feel my bones jar tomorrow as I plopped down on that hard deck.

"I've made about two hundred landings aboard," the chief went on. "So far I haven't had any trouble. Are you qualifying tomorrow, sir?"

I told him I was, if the carrier got down from San Pedro.

"Well," he said, "you won't have any trouble. Just watch Mr. Clark, and give yourself plenty of room when you turn into the groove. That's where most of the boys make their mistakes. They try to rush it a bit. It's not bad. You'll like it when we get out on the cruise and you get the hang of it."

He went on to tell me about operating around French Frigate Shoals and how once, back in the old days, he had had to bail out of a Corsair when a flying wire gave way. He had piled up in a cane field on the Island of Maui and scared the native Hawaiians half out of their sarongs.

We walked outside the hangar.

"You might win the cake tomorrow, sir. There is a thousandth landing due in the next group, and every pilot who makes one gets a big cake and has

AIR BASE

his name put up in the ship's deck ready room."

"That would be swell, chief," I said, "but I'll be satisfied to get aboard O.K. if it's only the nine hundred and ninety-ninth landing. Good night."

"Good night, sir. Good luck."

I made the rest of the rounds and then went back to the watch shack. It's funny how much you learn from the old hands at this game. By taking some of the advice with a grain of salt you find that your reaction in some ticklish situation is augmented by some little hangar gossip you've been in on.

The next day at noon the five of us took off on orders to rendezvous with the carrier, steaming north ten miles off Point Loma.

Chapter VII

A TYPICAL North Island day for the whole station is long and noisy. At about seven each morning the duty sections push the planes from the hangars to the parking places on the operating line. Just about this time the weather plane takes off for its long climb to high altitudes. At eight planes start taxiing down the line to the take-off area, and from then on an unceasing procession of take-offs and landings is made.

All day long the fighters, scouts, and bombers roar up and away to their practice areas or to any of the numerous auxiliary fields. Planes circle the island, towing their sleeve-gunnery targets behind them, drop the targets clear of the landing mats, and then come in to pick up new ones. On the bay seaplanes and flying boats dodge the shipping as they take off and land amid wallowing tugs, maneuvering destroyers, and anchored cruisers. In a less spectacular manner the overhaul shops are working at full speed to keep up with the pace the operating units are setting. About four thirty, all activity seems to stop as operations are secured until night flying.

Those who fly again that night shove off from their respective squadrons to have an early dinner and report back for flights that start at sundown. The shops close until the next day, though in the present emergency lights burn also until the night flights return. From sunset until ten the roar of powerful Cyclones and Wasps again abounds in the air as planes practice formation flying or make night-practice carrier landings on the field. Then, as the dead line approaches, the last pair of twinkling red and green lights comes swiftly down the bight, turns toward the mat, and presently the dim outline of a plane is silhouetted in the brilliant glare of the floodlights.

Its motor cut, the plane is quickly pushed into a hangar, the floodlights are extinguished, and quiet has again settled on America's busiest flying field. If four carriers are operating their squadrons at once from the base, business is extremely good.

(Official Photograph, U. S. Navy.)

Marine Fighting Squadron Two standing by for inspection at North Island.

(Facing page 102)

When these are out for cruises in and around the islands, up north to San Francisco, or down south along the Mexican coast, you find the Marine squadrons and utility groups taking over.

This morning, as the five of us lifted our wheels from the already warming tar to fly out to the carrier, we beat the usual rush by minutes.

"Take it easy, and bring them all back," Noz had pleaded as we left. "The cruise is too close to go hunting up new airplanes now. Save the crack-ups for the war games if you can, and don't forget," he added, "we were only joking about 'new bloods' cracking up the other day."

A hot sun had burned the ground fog off the island by eight o'clock, leaving a cloudless sky with perfect visibility. We were all excited about our first trip from the air station to land at sea aboard the *Lexington*, and I could almost have hummed a good song through the engine roar.

Gazing out past the clean silver fuselages and yellow wings that made up our V formation, I picked up the small nubs of land to the south that were known as the Coronados Islands. We often flew close to these crests of rock and scrub brush when going out to sea to fire fixed or free machine guns at target sleeves. The largest of these islands wasn't over a mile long and poked up out of the blue ocean some fifteen miles off the coast as though dropped there and forgotten. We were told that these islands were used by the Mexicans, to whom they belonged, for fishing retreats, but you could never spot any sign of habitation or any life except a few wild goats. Most early mornings, fog covered these "forgotten sea marks," but today they were sharp and clear outlines that broke an otherwise unmarred horizon.

Now, as we rounded Point Loma over the old lighthouse and headed out to sea, I felt that exaltation a man can feel on a cloudless day in a good plane. The radio cracked even as I made out the long white wake, trailing away in the blue Pacific behind the *Lexington*, miles out at sea.

"Two Baker Ten from *Lexington*—the ship is ready to land you aboard. Acknowledge!"

Lieutenant Stuart answered, "Aye, aye, from Two Baker Ten." I could now see the two plane-guard destroyers knifing along through the easy swells astern of the carrier on either side of the wake. Their purpose is exactly what their name implies. If a pilot lands in the drink near the carrier, one of these fast "guards" spurts out to give aid. They seldom miss, and in foul weather, with a heavy sea running, they literally plow through the rollers.

"*Lexington* from Two Baker Ten—we have the ship in sight and are waiting instructions," Stuart radioed.

Then he signaled, and we slid over into right echelon, ready to get down into the landing circle. As we passed over the carrier I could see the long, narrow deck alive with the men of the plane-handling crew. Black smoke was pouring out of her stacks on the superstructure. Aft at the stern I could just make out Sperry Clark getting squared away to signal us aboard. The ship piped up.

"Bombing Two planes from *Lexington*—land aboard!" I felt the tingle of something new and untried coming up as Stuart rolled away and headed out in a circle for the stern of the ship.

"Land aboard!"

That is the order you'll hear from Panama to Sitka, from Guam to San Pedro, from "Dago" to the Philippines when you start flying from the deck of a carrier. No matter how often those two words pipe up in your earphones, they will always give you a slight thrill. Land aboard! After hours of patrolling over unbroken sea or doing battle with the "enemy" in mock warfare, you get that order.

At once you unconsciously see the long sliver of a deck, the belching smoke, the scrambling crew, the long, trailing wake, flanked by the two whippet-like destroyers. At once you vision the steaming coffee in the wardroom, the soft leather cushion in your customary chair, the cribbage board and magazines, waiting down there after a long grueling flight.

Land aboard! I've heard it for days around Honolulu, Maui, Molokai, Lanai, Wake Island, and always with the same anticipation. It means put your wheels down—over the water, then over the deck, then on it. It means watch Sperry, try for a good smooth landing, see how straight and easy you can set her on the teakwood. It also implies that you *can* land aboard with no more than that short order, and subconsciously you are proud that it is taken for granted.

I watched over the side as our first plane went aboard and then, passing alongside the ship toward the bow, waited for Kane to break off. There he went! Out to the left in a wide circle, wheels down, flaps down, and hook down. I dropped my wheels, watched Kane. Then down went the hook and flaps, and I was in the circle heading for the groove. As I reached the destroyers behind the carrier, Kane hit the deck, and I slowed the plane down, got into the groove, and leaned over the left side of the cockpit to pick up Sperry. He was there, all right, his coat flapping against him in the manmade breeze blowing back across the deck. I was too fast. There. Gosh, that deck looked narrow! It felt as if we were moving pretty fast to land into some arresting gear and stop short. The stern heaved about a little in slow but firm oscillations, and I began to think about what the chief had said the other night at security watch.

"If the deck is coming up at you when you get the cut, ease it down. Don't push the nose over to duck into it."

Sperry had the come-on signal showing, so I must have been doing O.K. My left hand gripped the throttle as though even the pulsations in my wrist might change the angle of the arm in its quadrant. Almost to the stern now. The throbbing yellow ramp looked suddenly very large, and the signal officer was almost under the left wing. Below, the white-chopped wake from the ship's screws had become a scrambled and wider break in the blue sea. As I crossed the ramp I could make out two men behind Sperry, ducked low beneath the deck guard, watching and waiting, with microphones hooked around their chins. More deck crew was hunched over the side up forward, peering at the plane from the safety net some five feet beneath the landing platform.

There was the cut! Sperry jerked the paddle across his throat, and I could just catch a quick smile on his lips and nod as we flashed by. Pulling off the throttle, I eased the nose forward, then up a little, and we were on the deck. The arresting gear took hold immediately as the plane plumped to a sudden stop. I sank back away from the belt and swallowed my heart. Someone motioned hurriedly, "Taxi forward, taxi forward," as I sat there for a brief moment trying to gather my wits.

We were aboard. Only a few short minutes ago I was air-borne, circling above a blue ocean, attached to nothing. Now the throb of the straining ship's engines came up through the landing gear from the deck, up through the seat to nudge the parachute I sat on, as if to say, "Move on, boy, move on. There is someone who wants to sit down coming up the groove behind you." I was completely tickled, and taxiing up the deck past the rows of odd-colored sweaters of the deck landing crew, I masked a stern face to hide my childish glee. I thought to myself, "You made it O.K., you old son of a gun. Now you're a full-fledged carrier flier with one landing to your credit. Hurray!"

In the ready room below the bridge at the forward end of the superstructure, we sat around on the long leather bench seats, admiring our newly acquired "living room." Up against the wall on one side was the roll of names below the plaque that stated that these officers and men had negotiated thousandth landings aboard the carrier. The list was impressive, and I noticed the names of several of my old instructors at Pensacola sprinkled through the list. Bright brass, shined to high heaven, formed most of the fixtures, ash trays, cotton holders, and so on, that lined the walls. The deck was spotless, and I began to know what made Uncle Sam's Navy ships the cleanest in the world. It took a lot of swabbing to make that deck look like my mother's kitchen!

Outside on the wind-swept landing deck the

handling crew was rushing about, spotting our planes for take-off, gassing, and oiling the last few aboard. Sperry stepped into the gangway as we somewhat excitedly reflew our landing for the benefit of any "unfortunate" individual who might not have witnessed the feat. Not a mishap in the group. We felt kinda proud.

"O.K., fellows," Sperry said. We crowded around him to get the news. "Stuart, you were too slow obeying the signals. Speed it up, and don't go to sleep in the groove. Ewers, you were far too close to the right-hand side of the deck. Get lined up when you turn in at the destroyers, and then follow a straight flight path to the ramp. You'll end up in the stacks someday, sliding over there. Watch it on your next landings."

Sperry paused to flip the pages in his little notebook and then finished off the remaining qualifiers. He had mistakes for all of us to correct, and it brought us back to earth again after the elation that had blossomed in our bosoms while crawling out of our planes. Still, we were pretty happy about the successful qualifications and were anxious to get back to Alex and the squadron to tell them we hadn't scratched a plane and had all done O.K.

After a cup of coffee and a sandwich, thoughtfully brought up by the mess boy, the ship's loudspeaker sounded. "Pilots, man your planes! Pilots, man your planes!" We crawled back into our cockpits, warmed up against the chocks, and waited for the ship to swing back into the wind. Up forward the wave-off man was unfurling his checkered flag and scanning the deck to see that all was clear.

"Turn it up and hold your brakes!" The wave-off man signals his orders by flag. "Open your throttle wide." There. He puts a cupped hand to his ear and then looks at you. That means, "Your engine sounds O.K. to me. How about it? Are you satisfied for take-off?" Quickly you take a last look at oil temperature, pressure, manifold, tachometer readings. O.K.

A quick nod back to him, and he swings his starter flag. That's you! Off go the brakes, and the plane literally jumps forward. Down past the nose the end of the deck looks awfully close. Good God, do I have to get into the air in that space? you think to yourself. Over the end you can see the whitecaps flying spray from the ocean fifty feet below the bow. Straight down the yellow lines for the end of the deck. Then the wheels leave the deck as you ease back on the stick, with upturned faces flashing by and guns, nets, and bow drifting back and away. Then the ocean is under you. The deck falls away and gets play size as you pick up your wheels and turn out for the rendezvous.

What a thrill! It was worth all those hard, trying days back in training and then some to know that you could fly a fast fighting plane aboard an aircraft carrier far at sea, pick up fuel, bombs, ammunition, or what you needed, and then take off again to "go get the enemy." In the following years that I spent aboard the air station at North Island, I can picture time after time the qualifying groups of fliers returning from their first crack at deck landing at sea. They would gather around the lounge that night, as we did, and go over their "big moment"—their first carrier landing. You soon learn, even on cruises, long or short, that this type of gossip never grows old. You can't talk about it enough.

"Did anybody crack up?" was the first question

Bud asked when we sat down at the lounge that night.

"How many wave-offs did you get? Was the ship pitching any?" We answered all questions and by using hand motions explained just what happened and how we did it—needless to say, to the joy of some of the older pilots.

"Boy, did I drop in on the second one! I think old Sperry was trying to see how slow he could bring me in. I'll bet I didn't fly twenty feet forward after the cut. The old bus took it, though it sure jarred my backbone when we hit."

"Well, you know," Kane put in, "on my first two I had a hell of a time seeing the signals over the cowl flaps. My engine was heating up, and let me tell you, it's a job to peep around those open flaps without flying up the groove in a skid."

Before we ended our little hangar session half the new bloods in the lounge were gathered around listening in and, with a casual awareness, were picking up pointers on what can and does happen on landing aboard. Several nights before we had done the same thing, but it was quite pleasing now to act a little nonchalant about the whole thing and be the proverbial veteran aviators.

Throughout the next two days other squadron groups took off from the base to fly out to sea and land aboard in preparation for embarkation on the cruise. Big three-place torpedo planes, moderate-sized bombers, tiny, stubby fighters roared away from the field in groups and headed for the carrier. In the evening we would get the news.

"Stinky Davis sure put one away today. Hit the ramp coming aboard, and Stinky and one-half the plane slid on up the deck while the other half hung over the stern. Wasn't even scratched, the lucky rascal! Imagine!"

"Hear about Charlie? He must have doped off on his second landing and ended up minus landing gear and propeller. He's O.K. except for a big shiner and four stitches in his chops where the instrument panel didn't give."

We listened to the tales with avid interest and were just a little proud all the while that our outfit had come through unmarred. Ewers had made the thousandth landing and would receive the cake when we got aboard the next week to start the big cruise. Of course, he had to write home about that, and you couldn't blame him. We were a part of a big force of men, all pulling together like some huge football team, and though this was no longer play it was still much like a game in which you put out your level best to make the whole team better.

He usually doesn't like to admit it, but the pilot flying a fighting plane with his formation in the service, the bomber or fighter pilot going aboard the carrier still has his little tales to "write home about." There is still something about this flying game that holds it, as a profession, just a bit apart from others and allows all those who make flying their business to see eye to eye on a certain "something." In the service that "something" is known as *esprit de corps*, and although a member of a squadron may not detect this at first, he will soon recognize the existence of the unpopularized "think of your shipmate" phrase.

Probably the best illustration of loyalty up and loyalty down, so to speak, was brought out when Ensign Gil Brown, a reserve in the class behind us, stayed with his plane one day over the desert to give the enlisted man in the back seat a chance to bale out. Gil was ferrying a JF-2 Grumman Amphibian back to San Diego from Tucson, Arizona, with a third-class mechanic riding in the rear seat. Over the rugged, copper-colored Mohawk Mountain Range near Yuma, Arizona, where houses are still some forty miles apart, the engine suddenly became very rough. Before Gil could pull the throttle completely off the propeller let go and pulled off of the crankshaft. Within a short second or two the whole engine vibrated itself out of the plane and fell away. It all happened in a flash.

Gil jammed the stick forward to try and keep the now nose-light airplane in normal flight, at the same time yelling to the mechanic to bale out. After a few seconds more Gil pulled himself half out of the cockpit and started over the side, when he noticed the mechanic still struggling to get free of the plane. He dropped back down in the seat and grabbed the controls shortly thereafter, feeling the ship pitch as the mechanic got free and successfully opened his big silk umbrella. Then Gil started out again.

But he had waited too long. The ground was only a few hundred feet below now, and there wasn't a prayer of getting a chute to open fully in that space. He slid back into the seat, maneuvering the engineless ship as best he could until it crashed into the sandy desert to fold up like an accordian. That crash, by the laws of physics or what have you, should have cost Gil his life—and it almost did. He went through the subinstrument board, the half-intact part of the fire wall, and carried rudder bar and stick with him.

When the mechanic, who had landed some half a mile away, dragged himself to the plane over sand and cactus with a broken leg, he finally managed to get Gil out of the tangled wire and instruments, stretch him out on his unused parachute to render what first aid he could under the circumstances. On top of that, he dragged himself to the highway, another mile and a half north, stopped a car, and got some help. I talked to the mechanic a few days later, when they let us in at the hospital.

"That last quarter of a mile was sure long," he said. "I didn't think I could go another inch through that hot sand, but I guess we can do a lot of things that look impossible when we have to. I just remembered that I kept a thinkin' to myself about the title to a story I read somewhere—'The Long Haul.' Seemed like all I could think of was 'the long haul, the long haul'."

Gil was all messed up. His right elbow is now such that he can bend his arm only enough to get the hand in his pants pocket. One ankle is likewise stiff for keeps, and Gil has flown his last airplane for Uncle Sam. I believe the Navy sent him to a Reserve base for duty not involving flying, but I remember his words when he came over to the lounge for a drink with the boys after the hospital let him out for the first evening. We were all tickled to see him, though it was a shock to observe the drawn face, lined with stitches, the stiff arm in a cast, and the hop-hop as he carefully maneuvered across the linoleum on a pair of crutches.

"Listen, you guys," he said, "I know what you're thinking, and don't give me any of that stuff. I don't need sympathy or pity—so stuff it, will you? Who wants to roll for a drink?"

We all knew he meant it, too, undramatically and definitely, and we listened to his story of how it all happened until the officer of the day came around to take him back to the hospital. Gil lauded the enlisted man's sheer guts to high heaven and credits him with saving his life, which he certainly did. We all remembered, too, that Gil stayed with his plane to give his passenger the first chance. The boys at North Island won't forget soon the time the officer and the enlisted man saved each other's lives out there in the broiling sun and barren desert.

(Official Photograph, U.S. Navy.)

Four of the United States Navy's "floating airfields." The U.S.S. *Lexington*, followed by the *Ranger*, *Saratoga*, and *Enterprise*.

Chapter VIII

WHEN you first come aboard an air base to live for three or four years, you probably don't consider how much a part of its plan and organization you will become. As the months roll on and chance acquaintances grow into bound friendships on the field itself or in the town that supplies it, you begin to realize when the "cruise leaves for four or five months" you are leaving "home." Bud helped me pack the night before we shoved off. His Marine squadron was staying at North Island to practice gunnery while we were away, and for once they would have the entire West Field to themselves.

"Look, chum," he said, "don't forget to send me a couple of shots of those brown-skinned beauties out there. And remember, if we go out next year I want to have a couple of dates all lined up."

"You don't want much, do you, Bud?" I said.

"Well," he said, "you might roll one up in pineapple and ship it back here, grass skirt and all. Now, that wouldn't be much trouble!" We finished stuffing the last trunk, climbed into some makeshift, shipwreck clothes, and went over to the officers' lounge on South Field to take in the last get-together dance and free-for-all. It was called a "shipwreck party," and it is that literally when it ends up. It is the send-off with due hilarity that the boys throw for themselves at North Island prior to big cruises. When the fleet returns—if it has been to Hawaii—they toss what is called a "Hawaiian party," which serves the same purpose.

Naturally, since the present war has been going on in Europe, with forebodings running rampant in the Pacific, the old-time "big cruise" is changed to an almost continuous procession of ships and carriers in and out of the base. At the present time no one except the few who should knows of the whereabouts of our fleet and Naval Air Force, and the reason is obvious. Uncle Sam's first line of defense would be a poor "offense" if every other nation in the hemisphere could trace on a map our operations at sea. So the ships, carriers, cruisers, battleships, and destroyers slip in to San Diego Bay, San Pedro, San Francisco, and other points of service on the West Coast at odd times and intervals. They slip out and are gone in the same way.

"Hello, there, you two musty steers, come on and join the party," yelled Mike Chambers over the blat of a fair-to-middlin' colored band that was sending its best from one end of the long, high lounge. We went over and joined Mike's party. Mike Chambers, Second Lieutenant, United States Marine Corps Reserve, is probably the luckiest man flying, and he knows it. What happened to Mike about a month after he had arrived at the air station happens to the Spitfire boys in England daily now since the war started over Britain. And either they get superhuman for a few moments or the R.A.F. is short another pilot.

Mike had been up dogfighting with a scout bombing plane, an SBU-1, and, finding that he wasn't getting any pictures with his camera gun, Mike got a little overzealous.

"I swung around in a high turn to come back straight at him," Mike said. "Then I guess we both got the other in our sights at once, because the first thing I knew there was an SBU-1, big as all jolly hell, filling up the whole ring in my telescope. I squeezed out some pictures and then looked up fast, thinking maybe it was time for one of us to make a move, and—jumpin' fish—there he was!"

All Mike's flying mates were gathered around in the Marine ready room that day as they brought him back, parachute and all. The atmosphere was tense until Mike started telling the story, for all the boys knew what a nasty, close call he had had. But when he began to rub his funny-looking mop of sandy hair, with that "damned if it wasn't annoying" look on his face, the boys just couldn't keep the smiles down. When old Mike told a story, even if it was about his last haircut, he always got serious, almost lost the fight expression on his map, and worked in close to you while he elucidated.

"All I could do was pull the stick over all the way and hope the pilot of the scout would roll the other way. Well, he did, but we had waited too long. I felt a hard jolt and a good sock on the kisser and woke up hanging on the belt, hunched forward against the instrument panel. From there on it was anybody's game."

When they hit the two planes were at ten thousand feet over Otay Mesa. The scout had lost an entire wing tip and part of the tail, and both pilot and mechanic bailed out shortly after and got down O.K. But Mike had a different problem. The whole *left wing* of his fighter folded back over the cockpit, pinning Mike in like a new-fangled rat-trap, and the plane went immediately into a vicious spin. Mike heaved and strained against the wing, trying to force himself out of the cockpit, but every time he got his head and shoulders out the spinning motion of the ship flung the wing back again.

At something like four thousand feet he finally got his shoulders through and, hanging out over the side, watching the earth spin around like a top, tried to pull his feet through. They were all tangled up in the twisted mass of control wires. "I began to get awful mad," Mike said. Then he had kicked and jerked, pulling off the shoe that was fouled in the cables, and got everything out of the cockpit but his fanny, which was stuck where the paracute wouldn't quite come through the gap left between the wing and fuselage. The two occupants from the scout watched his plane as they floated down. "I didn't think he had a prayer," Jackson, the pilot, said. "It looked like his plane was almost to the ground when I saw his chute open. I'll swear he didn't have three hundred feet left." (Opening a parachute below five hundred feet leaves a lot to be hoped for. It has been done, but it's a squeeze play.)

Mike said he hit the nice soft dirt on the mesa, where some "wonderful farmer was plowing," and just lay on his back for a few minutes, completely relaxed. Then he got the farmer to haul him back to North Island, checked in at sick bay to get the punch in the nose fixed up, and strolled into the squadron room. And he never could figure out how he got his parachute free, nor did he remember pulling the rip cord. We teased Mike a little about leaving his plane and bailing out on such a "slight provocation," but after a look at the charred mass of scrap that the survey gang had hauled into the back of the hangar we knew how lucky he had been. Out in the fleet, when a fellow comes that close, we say he is "living on borrowed time."

By three in the morning we figured it was time to shove off and get some sleep. There were still crowds of "shipwrecked sailors" standing around in groups, singing the usual Navy songs that go with almost any party. We held up our corner until the last.

> Bell-bottom trousers, coats of Navy blue,
> He wants to climb the riggin' like his daddy
>   used to do.
> And if it is a girl then bounce her on your knee.
> But if it is a boy then send him off to sea.

Of course, there are variations that go along with all the songs. The later the party, the more variations. The admiral or commander, fleet air detachment, must have known about the evening frolic. Our orders weren't to fly aboard until two the next afternoon.

At seven the following morning the destroyers and cruisers started to slip quietly out of the bay. They filed out Indian fashion, in a long unbroken line, through the narrow channel that separates North Island from Point Loma, out around the old Spanish lighthouse toward the open sea. Crowds of wives, families, and relations lined Ocean Beach in the damp, gray early-morning mist, straining to see "papa's" ship as it stole out around the breakwater, freshly painted, in top shape for the war games. Before many of these officers and men aboard the ships would get back home, they *would* be proud papas. Three of the officers aboard our carrier were first-time fathers before we left Pearl Harbor on the return trip. They had to pace the flight deck miles at sea under "darkened ship" while the blessed event took place.

By noon we had our planes rolled out on the line, baggage stowed, and all gear securely lashed down. Lyons performed one of his usual miracles and had made everything shipshape, repainted insignias, had the planes scrubbed down and thoroughly checked and inspected. An officer doesn't usually have to help push the airplanes to the line, since it isn't his job, but now most of the ground crew had already gone aboard with duffel bags on a barge loaded with spare parts, so we all lent a hand. As soon as one squadron up the line finished pushing their planes out on the apron they went along to the next one, and so on down the line, until our four carrier squadrons were spotted, chocked, and ready to turn up. Across the field, past the new operations tower, the *Saratoga* and *Ranger* groups were busy spotting their planes, the yellow wings and silver fuselages shining in the noonday sun.

Bud came down from his squadron to see us off. We sat down in the dismantled ready room to have a coke and a game of cribbage, and the rest of the officers stood around outside or sat in their cars talking to their wives and families. The place seemed deserted, and the ready room reeked with a "to-let" atmosphere. Only the long table, without its green cover, the chairs, coffee mess near the bare windows, and the blank schedule board hanging at one end of the room remained. The captain was sitting in his office at the other end when the phone rang, and a few seconds later he came out, pulling on his jacket and wrapping his scarf around his neck.

"O.K., let's go. Someone find McClure and round up all the officers."

As we stood around pulling on flight gear and life jackets, Alex gave us the dope.

"The *Lex* is off the Coronados Islands about fifteen miles due west. She is heading 335 degrees true, making good a speed of 18 knots. Work out your problem for contact on your plotting boards, and man your planes in fifteen minutes. We'll cruise as usual at 150 knots, 8,000 feet. After the squadron is joined up over the lower bay, I'll circle left—we will rendezvous on Fighting Two. Any questions?"

There were none. We worked out our problem and started out to the line past the crowds of officers' families who were sitting in their cars around the hangars of the different squadrons to watch us get off. I guess it is quite a sight to watch some twelve squadrons of fighting planes roar out of a field by divisions, to join up finally in one huge, sky-darkening mass and head out over the ocean. And the crowds at the field knew that the group commanders would lead their groups in a farewell salute back over the Island just prior to departing for the ship. It is sort of a parade gesture, and we always liked it, always stuck our wings in nice and close and tried to make our squadron formation stand out above the others. It's all part of the game.

"Take good care of 'Hotdamn' Basil, you old landlubber," I yelled to Bud as we manned our planes and started the engines. I could just imagine how quiet the base would be about half an hour from now, and until the fleet returned. The Marines and a utility squadron or two would be left aboard the base. I could also imagine what a lot of fun the boys who remained behind would have with the officers' lounge all theirs in the evening and the pick of the female populace for dates. They loved it.

We ran up our engines, checking them carefully, and then followed Alex down the line out onto the field. Noz raised his hand, as Bill Kane and I edged up into position on his wings, and then we were off the mat, out over the Spanish Bight, and swinging down for the lower bay, climbing as we went, almost passing over the huge, sedate structure of the Hotel Del Coronado. You could pick out the crowds of people and automobiles that lined Ocean Avenue along the sea wall and see their upturned faces. There were probably some dismayed looks down there. The businessmen of Coronado almost close up shop when the cruise leaves, for nearly half the population has gone with the ships. It is a good time for their vacations.

"*Lexington* group from group commander, close up on me."

I looked up for a second over Nuessle's head and down past the skipper's plane. Immediately in front of our squadron were the eighteen planes of Scouting Two, preceded by the stubby Grummans of the Fighting Two "Hotshots." Ahead of them I could just make out the group commander's plane, flanked on either side by his protection—a section of single-seater fighters. A quick look behind showed the turtlelike bellies of the TBD's (Douglas torpedo planes), stepped up in formation above and behind our last section. The big three-place torpedo planes were massive hunks of wings and fuselages that lumbered along, high and undisturbed, menacing and powerful.

A torpedo plane is to a single-seater fighter what a battleship is to a destroyer, and though their medium for destruction is different they represent in the air force what the battle wagon does in the fleet. Just as submarines, destroyers, light and heavy cruisers, mine layers work on the sea for the protective scouting and defense work the battleships need, so do the fighters, the scouts, and the light-attack bombers act as guards, searching parties, and smokers in front of the heavy bombing and torpedo-carrying planes.

Now the group commander swung left in a lazy, sweeping turn, to allow plenty of room for the four eighteen-plane squadrons behind, and then, as the individual squadrons closed up into a solid group formation, he led us back over Coronado toward the Coronados Islands. I chanced quick looks down past the wing at the town. We were at six thousand feet, and I could make out the kids waving along the avenues, the officers' families still filing out of North Island in a stream of cars heading for home —where they would await daddy's return some three or four months hence.

We swung close aboard the beach that borders South Field, over the officers' club, where people were basking around the swimming pool and playing tennis in the early afternoon. You couldn't help feeling just a little pang of wishfulness as you gazed down on the spot that had become so well known and so chock-full of flying, so pleasant and exciting on gay evenings and athletic afternoons.

Not that every day is just eight hours of fun. It isn't. There are some rugged moments to be spent aboard an air base. Some days you sweat and swear behind a hot, howling engine, watching the section leader's head, wondering if you will ever land and get out of that cramped cockpit. Other days, you shiver and freeze beneath all the furs and flight gear you can get on; or streaming rain will whip back over the cockpit to dribble down through the cabin, splattering in your eyes and face, as you stare hard out over the cowl at the plane ahead.

Sometimes I wondered why in tarnation I ever got tangled up with flying and swore that the first chance that came along I would chuck it and take up farming. Then the next day the sun comes up bright and cheerful, and you actually want to sing as you lift your trim little fighting plane from the ground and reach up into the crisp spring morning for a cloud.

We used to sit around and discuss just what we were going to do when our tour of duty with the Navy was over.

"There is one thing certain," one fellow would say. "I'm finished with aviation as soon as I complete these four years. Boy, I'm going to work for my dad back in Ahlbedamned, Ohio, and forget I ever saw an airplane."

Another would say, "My bonus is going to set me up in the photography business, where I won't ever have to nurse a Cyclone again, with my ears stuffed with cotton."

I have to laugh now as I think what six of the fellows who were in my class, aboard my carrier for the entire four years of duty with the Navy, felt so certain of. I made notes of what they said and laid them away, just because each one of them was so all-fired bent on getting out of aviation when his time was up. Now, as I pick up the list again, I spot them in the following positions.

Gus Watkins, captain of an Eastern air liner, flying daily runs out of New York; Ralph Garrison extended his tour of duty—still flying for Uncle Sam; Chuck Rogers, copilot with Eastern Air Lines; John Hoyt, civil aeronautics inspector, flying every day; Bob Ewers, now a captain with TWA air lines; Peabody, chief test pilot for Pratt and Whitney engines. Those were the boys whose hearts and souls were *not* wrapped up in aviation as they got to know it aboard the air station at North Island!

As we neared the *Lexington*, which was digging her eight hundred and eighty-eight feet through the Pacific swells, the ship's radio came through, giving the sequence of the squadrons for landing. Each group acknowledged, and Fighting Two started for the groove, breaking into sections and then into the single-plane circle. Sperry was waiting with his signal paddles, and soon I was dropping my wheels and flaps, lowering the hook, and cutting in front of the destroyer, to land aboard with a hard bounce.

Then on with the throttle, up the deck past the barrier, to clear the landing platform for the next plane, and as the parking man signaled me into a spot I cut the switch. The last plane was coming aboard before I was out of the cockpit. He hovered, seemingly for several seconds, over the rising stern, then dropped solidly to the deck as the landing gear spread and the plane's landing gear squatted to take up the shock.

The siren sounded from the "island." The "island" is the nickname for the superstructure on the starboard side of the carrier, composed of smokestacks, the bridge, gun turrets, and ready room. We were all safely aboard.

Flanking the carrier on either side at several thousand yards were several destroyer divisions, followed by three light cruisers. Up ahead were the *Saratoga* and the *Ranger*, the other two carriers that had already taken their planes aboard and joined the main battle line. Far ahead were the battleships that were in standard cruising formation. They had shoved off from San Pedro earlier in the day to merge with the rest of the fleet before dividing for the war games. The sun was dropping into the ocean, red and glowing in the west, as we received the word to secure operations for the day. We went below to our rooms, arms loaded with chart board and handbags. The battle line swung into the sinking sun, and the carrier rolled along in place, as North Island, the coast line of California, and the distant mountain peaks fast disappeared. The ships bell clanged, one—two—three bells. The big cruise was on!

Chapter IX

"Man all flight-quarter stations! Man all flight-deck fire stations! Man all torpedo stations!" The loud scream and shrill bos'n's whistle blared out in the early morning as we piled out of our bunks, donned flight gear, and rushed for the lower ready room.

It was our third morning out, and the war was on. On the second day the fleet had split up into two parts, the black and the white, and now, as the dull, gray dawn broke through the portholes on the morning of the third, we—the whites—were ready to give battle. The carrier *Ranger* was designated as the air force of the black fleet, backed by all the scouting units of the battleships and cruisers in the black battle force. The *Saratoga* and *Lexington* were part of the white fleet, and we were ready to operate.

Inside the wardroom, which was rapidly filling with flight officers in flight gear, our skipper was counting noses and passing out slips of paper, showing us what was up. Three light cruisers had been spotted by our outer screen, and the ship was going to launch planes on a scouting line to pick them up and bomb them. Over in one corner of the ready room the radioman, with his earphones held close, was calling out the reports as they came down from the bridge. We hurriedly plotted courses to the enemy and back to the carrier on our plotting boards, gulping hot coffee and munching doughnuts as we figured.

Alex had passed around the news on the white and black fleets, on their respective strengths and disposition, as he had received it from above, and we knew after several conferences that were held during the first two days what the enemy was up to and why and what we were going to do about it for the next few weeks while the battle was on.

The roar of the warming motors sounded from the flight deck above as plane captains manned their planes, unfolded wings, and, on signal, started the engines for a quick warm-up check. When they were all set the switches would be cut and not started again until the respective pilots were at the controls. It doesn't take long to figure out just why, either. With some seventy or more airplanes stacked close together it isn't healthy to try to crawl around under and between whirling steel propellers—especially on a slippery deck, still dark and shadowy, with a chart board and pencil in one hand and a twenty-five mile wind blowing down the deck.

The skipper got the latest information as to what we would do after joining up.

"Scouting Two is taking off in ten minutes," he said. "They will scout ahead of us in the area where the enemy cruisers were last sighted. We are to follow them. On contact we will attack, dive-bombing by single planes. The rendezvous afterward will be ten miles astern the last ship in the enemy formation. I will circle left at four thousand feet. Number Eighteen will inform Torpedo Two by radio when the attack is completed." That was me. "And remember," Alex added, "there will be no voice transmission unless in extreme emergency. All reports in code."

The ready room was already half filled with smoke, and there was a tenseness in the thick air, as though this were actual warfare and not the beginning of the annual fleet maneuvers. These last-minute instructions in the ready rooms, the last cautions and reports handed to us, all seated around green-covered tables, the disposition of forces as set down on the blackboard by the air officer—this final episode always reminded me of the last-minute talk the coach used to give us just before we ran out on the football field. We used to think the coach's life depended on our winning the game and following his instructions, and the whole team would drink in every word with little more than a stir. Now the game had changed, but the team was here and the coach, and the same nervous anticipation ran through the eager-to-go group.

"Bombing Two, man your planes."

The loud-speaker blared across the room, and our table moved as one. We hurried out the nearest passageway and up the gangway and ladder that would bring us out on a platform just below flight-deck level. Scouting Two was already taking off. A plane would roar down the take-off area, over the edge of the bow, and up in a climbing turn. A few brief seconds of comparative silence. Then *r-rrrrruuuuuum*. The next would follow, and so on.

When we reached our planes, the scouting squadron was all clear, and you could just make out the forms of wings and fuselages as they gathered together over the ship like a covey of quail and were gone. Then we filed up the deck, single-spaced, moving slowly. The starter officer signaled, "Are you satisfied with your engine for take-off?" A nod. "Well, then, get it out of here," he seems to say as he signals for the take-off. Off come the brakes, up comes the tail, and you're off the deck, picking up the wheels, setting the propeller pitch, looking into the early dawn for the man ahead of you, to join up with the squadron.

It seems that whenever you get in the air to go out and attack the enemy you want to hurry the whole thing up a little, to get there and get at him, to send back that report, "Destroyed enemy force by dive-bombing attack and am returning to the ship."

After flying formation for so long, staring at the back of the section leader's head and his plane, you find yourself thinking of odd things that can fill up the grinding minutes and tiresome watch. I have found myself with absurd and playful thoughts many times while flying a grueling formation over an endless track of sea, hour after hour, watching the section leader, who, in turn, was tirelessly following the section below him. Was he as cold as I was? He didn't show it. My gosh, Noz, I would think to myself, turn around and stick your tongue out, thumb your nose, do something, anything. I've been looking right through the back of your leather helmet for two hours and ten minutes, and you haven't turned around once, not once. Not only that, but you don't look cold, and I'm shivering like an old woman.

Then my thoughts would stray as I tried to figure out what was happening back at the base right now, what our next port would be like, and whether I ought to blow my whole pay check at once or spread it out to make a big splurge at San Francisco when we got back. From that point I could think of anything from what I could get out of life as an aviator when Navy duty was over to designing a finish for the *Unfinished Symphony!*

You have to. You can sit for perhaps an hour, moving the throttle, pressing the rudder bar, easing the stick. Then time begins to weigh heavily. You are used to every move the man leading you will make, and by predetermined motions the thing becomes almost automatic. Every hour after that first one, unless it is filled with maneuvers or broken by an attack, in which, for a time, you change speed, altitude, sounds, and position, well—every hour that follows seems like eternity. The sea below is endless, like the roar of the Cyclone up ahead.

It was a little over an hour when the crack of the radio in my ears made me jump with a start. Scouting Two, somewhere across that trackless blue water, had spotted the enemy. The tapping key was clear and sharp, and I scribbled down the message with one hand while flying with the other.

"Three CV's bearing 233 degrees, course 185 degrees, speed 15 knots."

Alex started to climb for altitude, and I knew it wouldn't be long. There wasn't a cloud in the morning sky now, and we would probably go up high, come in with the sun on our backs, and try to make the attack fast. We slid over into echelon, each plane dropping below the preceding one as we "stepped down," preparatory to pouring over into the dive to follow the leader. There they were! Three small objects ploughing along through the swells, making the only break in sight with their telltale wakes trailing behind. We were all set.

Alex wiggled his wings, rolled over, and started down. A sudden flash of silver and yellow, and the next plane rolled. Then the next and the next. I adjusted the sight, closed the cowling flaps tight, and pulled up on my safety belt, glad that there was some action coming. Noz rolled into a dive, and I followed right behind him. Down we went, stretching out in that long, steep line of diving planes, seemingly almost to the water just in front of the cruisers. It's a sight you see many times while flying in the fleet for Uncle Sam. I lined the third floating fortress in the sights, watched her superstructure grow suddenly larger and larger. Then I tripped the landing light (the substitution for a bomb in mock warfare) and pulled out above the belching stacks to trail Noz to the rendezvous point.

I wondered if Larue, the mechanic in my back cockpit, had blacked out on that one, and I turned around to see. He grinned back and made a circle with his thumb and index finger to mean, "Everything is O.K." Then I tapped out the message to Torpedo Two to tell them that we had completed our attack and were heading for the carrier. They would finish with a horizontal bombing attack, and that would be the finish of three enemy heavy cruisers. The white fleet had chalked up the first score of the year's war games.

Back aboard the carrier, we found the whole of Scouting Squadron Two awaiting our arrival in the lower ready room, and we sat around over coffee and hot sandwiches to discuss where the rest of the black fleet were, when they would attack us, and where the *Ranger* might be hiding. Before fleet problem twenty was over we were to find that the elusive little carrier *Ranger* was the black mark on our record. We never could find her and thus never could put the air force of the black fleet out of commission. She was like some pirate ship of old, yet maneuvering fast, launching her planes for lightning attacks on our battle line, and then skipping away to get her aircraft ready at some other vantage point. Her whereabouts became the talk of our whole fleet, and before we pulled up at La Haina Roads, off the island of Maui, I believe every man in the Pacific fleet was just a little proud that the *Ranger* and her crew were part of the United States Navy. We had a great time teasing the boys of the Scouting Squadron. Any time we wanted to "get in their hair" all we had to say was, "Does anyone know where the *Ranger* is?" It burned the scouters, because they spent a good part of their time scouring the sea for the enemy carrier, with about as much luck as the patrol outfits that were out after her.

For nearly three weeks the war went on at a hard pace. Ordinarily, when you go aboard an aircraft carrier for short cruises or practice landings, the day is spent in operating, flying off and back aboard, with a lecture sprinkled in here and there between flights. In the evening, around the wardroom after dinner, you sit down to read magazines, listen to the radio, play bridge, cribbage, or maybe a little penny-ante poker. There is always a movie immediately after dinner on the hangar deck, and if you have already seen *The Count of Monte Cristo*—well, you sit there and enjoy it again. Some of the afternoons you have no flight operations scheduled, no lectures or duties, and you put on a bathing suit to go up topside and lie in the sun on one of the guard nets stretched out over the water. It was, all in all, some work and some play.

But on this cruise, the big one, when the whole fleet was divided for several months' battle practice, we found that someone on Uncle Sam's naval staff wasn't joking. We were to simulate war conditions from start to finish. We did. Our days ran like this:

Up at two thirty in the morning to stumble through the dark-blue "battle lights" that showed you just about where the passageway should have been. Down to the ready room, in flight gear, ready to work out a navigation problem, learn the objective for the dawn flight, and get a general picture of the enemy's disposition of the moment. Then up to the plane and off by the first crack of light around the horizon, to fly for three or four hours, hunting down the opposing force. An attack, a hurried rendezvous, and then back to the ship to eat lunch and be ready for a flight within an hour. When flight quarters sounded, again you were back in the ready room, up to the planes, and again in the air for three or four more hours of formation flying on a protective patrol. By evening your parachute felt like a part of you, and sitting on anything else was strange. After dinner the lights were out for anything except maneuvering through dim, blue-lighted passageways to your room, and after a walk around the deck there was nothing to do but sleep.

AIR BASE

"Great day in the morning," Vensel, my roommate, would say, as he stumbled in through the darkened passage and fumbled in the dark to take his clothes off. "Do you suppose they will ever lay off of this 'darken ship' business and just say 'damn the torpedoes' like one of our famous Admirals did? If this blackout keeps up much longer we'll all be strangers."

Joe Vensel was a character in himself. With all his five feet five inches pulled up to fighting strength, little Joe "Beany" Vensel would just throw himself into anything that walked on two feet or four and never ask for quarter. He was the fireball of the outfit, a neat-flying, cagey little package of suppressed explosive. We called him "Beany" on the first day he hit the fleet from Pensacola, because his head was shaped like a lima bean.

"Just lemme hang one on 'm, Guy, just one," Beany would plead as I held him to prevent his being splattered by some six-foot giant who somehow had crossed him during the evening. "Hear what he said about me? I'll button his big lips, so help me, if you'll just turn loose of my swinging arm," he'd say.

And he meant it. Joe and I had been close friends ever since he hit the fleet, and when the two of us walked along together there was every reason for people to laugh. Joe and his bouncing five five, which couldn't boost a scale to a hundred and forty pounds if life itself depended on it, and my lumbering six foot three, which produced a fair-sized frame, was a funny sight. But you have a lot in common with a fellow you live with for three years. Especially if that living as shipmates requires sleeping in the next room on an air base, bunking for months on end in a matchbox-sized stateroom aboard an aircraft carrier, flying, eating, playing, worrying alongside one another like a couple of brothers.

As a flyer, there was none better than Beany, but one day I had to laugh at him despite our ticklish position. The incident is worth relating because, as so often aboard an air base, fate can be ironical and hard, as it turned out in this case. Sometimes you wonder. We had underestimated the magnanimity of a fog bank over the high Lagunas while returning from a cross-country flight to El Paso, Texas. There were five of us flying an opened-out V formation, and everything was going nicely. We rumbled along over Tucson, around the Gila River bend, and out across the Imperial Desert past Yuma, with perfect weather. We had been on the cross-country trip for two days, stopping in at Phoenix and Las Vegas, to acquire the usual experience that the air-base doctrine called for in the way of cross-country flying. Now, as Lieutenant Mead, leading the formation, made the last swing around Yuma, over the Colorado River, and edged along the Mexican border toward the mountains and North Island, we were all a little happy about getting back to the air station for Saturday night. Then, just as we passed over the dried-up town of El Centro in the heart of the desert we saw it.

Up ahead, blanking off the usual horizon of rugged mountain peaks and ridges, was the fog. It stood right at the edge of the desert, fifty miles from home, and mounted like a huge white wall, high and menacing. Weather reports had spoken of a two thousand-foot ceiling at San Diego, with broken clouds and "thick haze" over the mountains. All five of us saw the ominous-looking fog bank at about the same time, and unconsciously we closed up to await instructions. Vensel and I were flying the tail-end wing positions of the V.

Across the air space that separated our planes Beany slid his goggles up, pointed up ahead, and wrinkled his brow into a wry face as he shook his head. I nodded back and held my nose.

Lieutenant Mead piped up on the radio. "What do you think, fellows? Shall we go up high and go on through on instruments, or do you want to go back and land at Yuma? I just got the last weather sequence, and they still say North Island is two thousand feet, with broken clouds and light rain showers."

George, of course, had the final say as to what we would do, but like all good leaders he wanted the opinion of his followers. We thought it over. I knew that there wasn't a weather station up in the mountains. In fact, there weren't any weather stations between Yuma and San Diego. The radio beam, which cuts across the mountains from Lindbergh Field, had a bad habit of "swinging" at some points. We were almost at the fog bank, which closed off the mountain range like a curtain.

"Bunky" Ottinger, half-pint gunnery officer, broke the silence.

"Let's go on up to ten thousand and go on through," he said through the cracking static from

(*Official Photograph, U. S. Navy.*)

An endless track of ocean beneath their wings.

(*Facing page 150*)

his number two position. "Yeah," Larson put in from number three. "If North Island has two thousand feet and a broken overcast we can let down through that O.K." I could see Larson hold his microphone up to his lips as he talked. We were pulled in close. Vensel and I reported that it was O.K. with us. Then we were in the white blanket, climbing for that extra margin of safety and keeping our wings close in to the tail of the next plane in order to hold visual contact and not get lost.

Flying in fog is no fun. In fact, despite the dependable instrument-flying equipment of today, you still have to keep a positive and unfailing watch, a steady concentration on that black panel full of dials with dancing needles. One hour of being on instruments, seeing nothing beyond, nothing below, watching only the pointers in their cases with an occasional quick glance at the streaming-wet wing tips ploughing through white mist, and you have worked your brain hard. If you have ever walked along through a thick snow on a black night and tried to keep a sidewalk under you, you have a good idea of what flying in fog is like—except that you can't take time out to get your location all squared away before continuing.

"Don't anyone open up on the radio," Mead called through his microphone. "I'm going to tune in the beam now."

I chanced a quick glance through the murky whiteness at Vensel's plane. To my amazement, it was cocked up on one side, flying along in a skid, its silver belly glistening with wetness. I quickly reached for the mike and then remembered Mead was on the beam. Then I suddenly realized what Beany was doing, and I laughed to myself. He had obviously let his sense take charge and believed we were all flying in a skid so he was going to fly level! He felt that we were turning. His mind just wouldn't change his sense of feel. This can happen any time you are flying formation on another plane through fog or even on a dark night. It's a queer trick of the senses. Poor Beany. He hung right in there, one wing down, one wing up. Afterward, he swore we were the ones who were flying cockeyed —not he!

For one hour and twenty minutes we struggled along in the white-blanketed silence, the even drones of the engines seeming to blend with the stillness. The wet blast from the propeller would scatter across the windshield to drip down into my eyes and face. With one glove off, I mopped the drops away almost continuously. I wished we could see some holes and some ground. None of us heard about the lone plane that had taken off from Yuma about an hour after we went over. None of us knew that Lieutenant Forbes, ferrying a single-seater fighter—one of the stubby little Boeings—was following along behind us to try and come through the soup, also, and get home for Saturday night. If we had known about him, we would have radioed to try to stop him. As it turned out, the five of us were lucky. Forbes wasn't.

It was another half hour before we got into North Island. I know five Navy fliers who never want to repeat such a flight. We climbed to eleven thousand feet, twelve thousand, thirteen thousand. Still no break. Nothing but that vast whiteness enshrouding our five planes, so that the leader at times was hardly distinguishable through the stuff. Lieutenant Mead knew what he was doing, but he couldn't stop the weather.

"Just hit the cone of silence," he called through the mike. "We'll let down right over the field."

Then he called the base radio at North Island. "Two Baker Seven to North Island tower—five planes Bombing Two over the San Diego range station and letting down to get contact with the ground. How is the weather at North Island?"

I listened attentively, straining to pick up the message. It came in faint and blurred.

"North Island tower to Two Baker Seven—your message received. Land as soon as possible. Weather moving in from the west and ceiling lowering. It's now about twelve hundred feet, with no breaks, and raining steadily. Receipt."

George O.K.'d the message, and we started down. A glance over at Joe, and I could see that he had finally straightened out and was flying level. Down we came through the vast whiteness. Eight thousand, six, five, four, two thousand feet! We were below the mountain-peak height, still in the thickest fog I have ever flown in. I kept hoping that Lieutenant Mead had hit the cone of silence on the button, for if he didn't and the wind drifted us very far to the east—well, mountains don't move easily!

Then, just as I began to squirm, wondering when we would break through, a hole appeared dead ahead and below us, and through it we poured. For the first time in almost two hours we could see something besides that solid wall of white, could relax and look at something besides the plane ahead. At a thousand feet we picked up the rotating beacon at North Island, yellow and faint through the rain, and shortly after, the five of us—still in formation—sat down as one on West Field and splashed up to the line. Almost before we had reached the squadron ready room to see who was still there it was dark. The fog was right down, kneeling on the black tar, and we all huddled around to thank our lucky stars. We were all having a laugh on Beany and happily joking, now that the nerve-racking experience was over, when Alex walked in.

"Mead, why didn't you go back to Yuma and land when you found out how thick that stuff was?" he said.

"Well, I was going to do that, captain," George said, "but about halfway through the stuff I picked up the San Diego beam and decided to fly it on in. It was a clear and well-defined signal."

You could tell something was in the wind the way Alex looked. He laid a message down on the table. "Lieutenant Forbes, Scouting Two, was just forty minutes behind you, coming in from a ferry hop. He tried to come through, too, probably on the beam. A rancher just called Operations and said a plane crashed into the side of the mountain above Alpine and burned up. The plane number he got from the tail was 9088. That was Forbes."

You could hear a pin drop as Alex went on. "He was apparently flying the beam from the time he entered the fog bank, and the east leg had swung off over the mountain. If you had followed the beam all the way through from the desert we might have had five planes go into the side of that mountain." Alex looked hurt. "I'm glad you got through O.K.," he said, "but I'm sorry you took the chance." Then he went out.

I'll never forget the dumfounded, startled expressions that followed him. There had been nothing to say, nothing, and we sat for fully a minute in absolute silence, just staring out the window at the splashing rain beating down through the black night.

As we drove back to the officers' quarters I began to think what a lucky bunch of birdmen we were, and even Bud was serious about it as I related what had happened. Beany's "cockeyed" flying never seemed to be quite so funny after that. It was always shadowed by Forbes's crashing plane and the realization that only a stroke of good fortune had kept us from the same fate.

Chapter X

THERE's one thing about carrier operation for the pilot who is earning his bread and butter flying from one. Life is never dull. A pilot has to be on his toes every minute of the time he is aboard for fleet maneuvers, or the chances are good that he will find himself holding up the entire ship. When he takes his plane off the deck and when he comes back to land, not only his life but the lives of several of his shipmates are at stake. Some of the accidents that happen just can't be explained, and after a bad one you don't find much talk or long grieving about it. There isn't time. Such was the case during the second week of operations, when McLoughlin and Pickett went in off the starboard bow while their squadron was taking off.

I was flying Number Eighteen that day and had just joined up with the squadron as the last plane in the formation. Scouting Two were taking off just after us, and we circled back over the stern of the ship at four thousand feet to wait for them. There was a low haze, which extended up to nearly a thousand feet, and our squadron rendezvous had been cautious and slow, to eliminate, as much as possible, the danger of a mid-air collision. Just as the last four planes of Scouting Two were filing up the deck for take-off, the heartbreaking sound of "CRASH, CRASH, CRASH" screeched through the earphones. Almost at the same time, down past the yellow wings of our squadron, I saw a huge ball of black, ugly-looking smoke rising slowly from the water. I knew what that meant. There is something about smoke from a burning plane that you never mistake.

The radio again. "Two Sail Eleven and Twelve just crashed in the water about three miles, bearing 45 degrees on the starboard bow! They are both burning on the water!" It gave you a sudden shock like a dive into icy water. I looked over at Kane, flying Number Seventeen. He was watching that cloud of black smoke, too. Then he looked over and shook his head. I felt sorry for Bill right then. He had been in Scouting Two before being transferred, and he knew every man in it.

The air was alive with radio transmission between the carrier and the planes that were in the immediate vicinity of the crash as Alex led us out over the spot. The calls were somewhat tense and excited, and all radio procedure was disregarded. "*Lexington*, I am circling right over the spot. There is no sign of any of the occupants or the planes. I can make out what appears to be a piece of parachute a wheel floating free, and a piece of a wing."

Then the commanding officer of Scouting Two broke in. "The planes that crashed were Two Sail Eleven and Twelve. Number Ten stand by the crash spot until the destroyer arrives. The rest of Scouting Two join up on me."

Then the *Lexington* came in. "All planes stand by to land aboard."

A plane-guard destroyer was nearly at the spot, ploughing the seas like some mad porpoise. There was a spreading oil slick covering half a mile of water where the planes hit. Even from four thousand feet I could make out a crumpled wing and a piece of white cloth that must have been the parachute. What a tough break. Only two weeks out on the cruise and to have such a nasty accident! There were four men in those two Vought scout bombers—two pilots and two mechanics. We couldn't tell until after we had landed who it was, and the suspense was awful. You just sat there, dazedly flying your plane behind the section leader, trying to imagine who wasn't alive any more and how the damned thing happened.

After we had landed aboard, everyone filed silently into the wardroom. I quietly asked Luchtman, the navigation officer of Scouting Two, who it was and how it had happened.

"Pickett and McLoughlin," he said. "Mac was joining up in the section from the inside. Pickett had already joined up on the outside wing position. Mac must have squashed into him in the haze, trying to judge his distance a little too close. They didn't have a prayer. Only five hundred feet up."

There was no undue sentiment in Lucky's voice but, rather, a tone of shock and disrupted emotion. He didn't say anything more. The rest of his squadron was sitting around a table. Some of the boys were toying with their helmets, some just staring out the portholes at the gray mist that still hung over the ocean. And that is the way it happens sometimes. Everything going along rosy, everyone striving hard for an objective, and—plunk! The inevitable stretches up into your sky and pulls down a couple of your flying mates. Such misfortunes are the misfortunes of war, real or practice, and there is nothing to do but take it on the chin and keep your sense of humor. Maybe as we first arrived at the base we would have looked for a little sympathy when a shipmate was lost. We didn't now. We were hardened to the hardness of it. Kane came around that night, and we played our usual round of cribbage, but he was thinking back to his academy days and said very little. McLoughlin and Pickett were former classmates of his from Annapolis. Later he told me he used to wrestle with Mac on the wrestling team when they were plebes and that he had roomed with him while in Scouting Two. When the ceremonies were over the next day the *Lexington* got back into the thick of the war.

For two more weeks we pounded the ocean, flying from the first crack of light until dark. The carrier skipped in and out of the main battle line to launch planes; scout, attack, bomb the black fleet—our big-cruise enemy. Off we would go into the gray of early morning, follow the scouts to a disposition of enemy forces, and try to sneak through their protective patrol in order to score on their main battle line of heavy cruisers and battleships. At night, with all planes back aboard and the ship darkened to fleet blackout, our whole force would attempt to slip away at top speed and be ready to launch the attack from another point the following morning. The black fleet was doing the same. The best way Uncle Sam can be ready for an attack in his waters is to send his fleet out there, divide it like a baseball team, and give each an objective to accomplish. If either is successful, where is the weakness? Find it, return to the base for supplies, new personnel, new equipment, and then out to sea again to fight another "war." That's the why of an air base, and the cruises, war games, maneuvers, and even the cross-country flights around the United States are all a part of the training a pilot must go through to become efficient. There are no short cuts.

One day, as we were returning from an attack on two submarines that Scouting Two had kicked up and reported, an amusing incident took place that gave us many a laugh when the whole story came out. It seemed that Ensign Kelley, flying one of the big three-passenger torpedo planes, ran completely out of gas some fifteen miles from the ship. He dropped away from the squadron and started down, spotting a tramp steamer and gliding for that bit of refuge from the cold waters that lay below him. Kelley was the kind of man you couldn't help laughing at. He had a big Irish face, jovial and mischievous, knew so many jokes he could keep going for hours without a break, and was liked by everyone. As he neared the water he had almost reached the tramp, and his section leader, who had followed him down, reported his safe landing on the water.

The *Lexington* couldn't turn around and go after him, because we were all low on fuel and had to land aboard shortly. One of the plane-guard destroyers started over to play retriever. The tramp had noticed the plane in distress and had immediately stopped her engines, put out a boat, and taken the three aviators off their sinking plane. The flotation gear had functioned properly, and the bags had inflated, but before the destroyer got there to salvage the plane the choppy seas had carried it away, and the plane went down. The tramp steamer turned out to be French, out of San Francisco, and the captain entertained the three boys in no uncertain manner.

They went along to his cabin, where he proceeded to open up his choice wine stock. In order not to "embarrass" the captain, the boys drank some long and lusty toasts to everyone's health. Far be it from Kelley not to hold up his end of the Naval etiquette he had learned! After all, here was a captain of a ship saying "drink" to the United States, "drink" to France, "drink" to fortunes of circumstance! As a matter of fact, they were very happy to be guests of the Frenchmen—and very unhappy to leave.

When the destroyer finally arrived several hours later all three of the boys were in fine spirits. As they boarded the quarter-deck of the carrier you could hear the melodious voices of Kelley's trio wafted up even to the bridge. There were more amazed looks on blank faces that day than you have ever seen in one group. Kelley swears that if every forced landing turned out like that one, he would put in a bid for all of them! Whenever we gathered around to do some barbershop harmony after that, it was known as "Kelley's trio," or, as Vensel put it, "sour notes from sour grapes!" When you hear Kelley—his reddish cropped hair sticking up as if at attention—tell about his escapade, the result is even funnier.

As the cruise goes along and a necessary silence prevails on all maneuvers and results, unanswerable questions pile up.

"How many of the enemy ships does Commander Battle Force give us credit for destroying?" "How did those two submarines slip through the outer and inner screens yesterday?" "I heard that they got credit for sinking a heavy cruiser and three destroyers!" "Wonder where the *Ranger* is operating. Since that second attack her planes made on our carrier, there hasn't been any report of her location." "The officer of the deck told me that we will probably anchor at La Haina Roads day after tomorrow and take a breather."

And so it goes. You spend a lot of time at meals picking up the latest "guess" reports on how the "war" is progressing, asking timely questions, speculating as to the outcome. It becomes like a business organization, in which everyone is wondering whether business is good or bad. You don't

(Official Photograph, U. S. Navy.)

Performance of these huge "flying bombracks" is more than gratifying.

(Facing page 166)

know how the war is coming along while communications are silenced, reports censored, and hits or misses kept secret. I remember how it was in France in the first six months of the present war, how none of us knew where the Germans were, when they might attack, what the British were up to, or just how the Low Countries were holding out. What we had read in papers was little more than a feature writer's brain child, and that was pared and edited by censors. So it went in fleet maneuvers.

Now, out near the Hawaiian Islands, the black and white fleets closed in for the final stage of mock war that had started from the base at San Diego. The steady diet of early flights off the dew-covered deck, the endless track of ocean beneath the wings, the numerous conferences between flight operations, the darkened ship each night—all this became our whole existence.

"The black fleet is now believed to be somewhere in the vicinity of Johnston Island. Our position at present is here." The air officer would point to the map, indicating by the cardboard ships pasted along its lines just where we were and why we were doing *what* we were. Every pilot aboard the ship would be grouped around the tables of the wardroom during the conferences, trying to see what the war looked like on paper. It was getting hot as we neared the islands, and the smoke was thick, even with the ports swung wide open. "Remember, it is imperative that the strictest radio silence be kept. Any voice transmission at this point would be readily picked up by any ship listening in on that frequency, and any two enemy ships who heard us could get a radio fix at once."

Naturally, in any emergency, radio silence had to be broken, but one day we had a long laugh when a pilot in one of the planes left his radio switch turned to "communications" instead of "intercockpit." He thought he was talking only to his mechanic in the back seat, but every plane in the sky heard him as he shot the breeze with his mech to break the monotony of a long patrol.

"How did you meet your wife in the first place?" said the first voice, breaking the day's silence. "Oh, I knew her on the farm back in Missouri. She came out to Los Angeles to get a job about a year ago, and we started going around again. Shucks, one day I found myself buying a ring—and there we were!"

"Gosh, that's great," the first voice answered.

"Yeah, she's going to meet me in San Francisco when we get back."

Fortunately for them, they didn't mention any names. Consequently, no one ever found out who the culprits were.

"Tomorrow," the air officer would say, "we take off early again and form a scouting line first to try and pick up the *Ranger*. There will probably be three flights, with the last section of Scouting Two acting as the smokers for torpedo attack." (The "smokers" lay down a screen of white smoke around an enemy force to allow the torpedo planes to go in under cover and drop their "fish.") After about an hour or two the conference would break up, and we would pack our weary bones off to the cribbage board for a "quickie" and then straightaway to bed.

Besides all the flying, the conferences, and the interrupting enemy attacks (we always had to man flight-quarter stations during an attack), there were still the regular squadron duties to perform. As assistant engineering officer I had little time to waste. I had my hands full getting the dope from Lyons on the status of our planes, which were ready, which needed engine checks, what planes couldn't be flown that day because of cracked landing gears or bent propellers. It is a big job to keep eighteen planes flying every day, and Nuessle, Lyons, and I spent many hours figuring what crew could check what plane on the hangar deck and which planes needed new props or landing gears.

From dispatches sent around at long intervals we learned of the casualties that had occurred among our brother fliers on other ships. Jones, one of our class, a somewhat nervous, red-haired individual, who had always been conscientious about his flying, spun into the ocean after he rammed the mast of one of the plane-guard destroyers while he was getting into the groove to land aboard the *Ranger*. Jones hadn't been long enough in the game to learn by experience what he should have been on the alert for. Watching out the left side of the cockpit of his Grumman, he had failed to notice that he was drifting into the destroyer as he swung wide into the groove. The mast sheared the little Grumman's right wings, dropping both Jones and his plane straight down to Davy Jones's back yard. Only the two splintered wings were found, and the *Ranger* held sea services for a shipmate lost at sea.

The battle continued. On our carrier mishaps

frequently were hair-raising, but since Scouting Two's tragedy, they had not been too harmful to personnel. A Douglas torpedo plane hooked a wing in the edge of the curved ramp while trying to gain altitude after a wave-off. The plane dropped straightaway into the boiling wake of the carrier and disappeared. Less than a minute later, three heads popped up in the white froth, signaling that they weren't badly hurt. We all breathed a lot easier, for it had seemed that no one would get out of that one. The nearest "can" sped forward, dropped life preservers, and then lowered a boat to fetch aboard the three bruised aviators.

In our squadron, Ensign Ewers, a tall, clean-looking chap from Seattle, managed to pick out a clear spot on the "island" at the last stack and proceeded to make a crumpled pile of what had a moment before been a sleek, rugged-looking Vought dive bomber. Ewers only got bumped hard on the head, but the mechanic sustained a broken arm. In all, we were very lucky.

One morning before take-off we sat around the table in the wardroom after flight quarters had sounded, awaiting instructions as to what our mission would be, when the word got around that this was the last day of the "war." It was expected that the order to "cease all present activities" would be given at sundown, and everyone was in great spirits.

"I believe we are going into La Haina Roads late tomorrow afternoon," McClure said, as he handed out the yellow sheets for the pilots to sign. (Yellow sheets are the forms used by the Navy to show the status of an airplane before flight.) Colored mess attendants scurried around the tables answering last-minute calls for coffee. They always seemed to move silently when we came down to flight quarters in the morning; they obviously knew about a man's temperament in the early hours before breakfast.

"If we do," Mac went on, "it will probably mean that the whole aircraft and scouting force will anchor there to refuel and get set to enjoy a few days in Honolulu very shortly."

It was good news, and I noticed that afternoon, as we came back aboard from our last bombing hop, in which we had supposedly laid flat an enemy-patrol base on French Frigate Shoals, that the landings on the carrier were a little snappier than during the last few days. Even old Alex kicked over the traces a bit while we were on our way back from the shoals. Passing over a few straggling sand bars, which were poking out of the varicolored coral-painted ocean at odd spots, the skipper noticed on one of the strips a drove of huge turtles sunning themselves. We suddenly got the signal to slide over into echelon, followed by the attack signal. Down we came. Alex held the nose of his plane right on the backs of the lazy turtles, and seventeen of us poured down right behind him, engines gunning and propellers whining. We pulled out some fifty feet over the broad, shining backs, one after another, expecting to see the turtles splash into the water to escape what must have appeared to be certain death. To our amazement, there wasn't a stir among the bold critters, not even so much as a raised head or outstretched leg! When I pulled up again into formation, Nuessle turned around, scratched his head under his helmet, and looked askance at me, as if to say, "How do ya like that!"

That is the way Navy flying sometimes goes, and your skipper has a good reason for it. After all, he sits up there in the lead plane, figuring, estimating, planning, flying his plane, and leading his squadron into attacks and maneuvers. He feels the urge to kick up his heels, too, and when the proper time comes you may find yourself trying to hang in a "squirrel case," a pleasant follow-the-leader maneuver in which the skipper dives, rolls, Immelmanns, and loops, with seventeen fighting planes chasing along after him like a long line of skaters cracking the whip. Or, of course, you could be attacking a flock of mammoth turtles, around French Frigate Shoals, aghast when they almost yawn in your face as you scream by! It serves to break the tension of long patrols, and after weeks of pure concentration on the art of aerial destruction you are happy to whip around the sky a bit for the "sheer hell of it."

By four thirty we were back aboard the ship, and at five fifteen the *Lexington* swung back onto the battle line to prepare for dropping anchor in La Haina Roads off the island of Maui. Down in the officers' mess a radio was twanging out lazy Hawaiian music. Until we left Honolulu some two weeks later, the war was over, and after hurrying through dinner we all scrambled up on the flight deck to watch the land come into sight.

There is a marked difference between seeing the

Hawaiian Islands from the deck of a ship as she swings into port, and flying near them, glancing down past a wing to pick out, several thousand feet below, what spells Hawaii on your chart. For the last few days our mock battles had lead us around the islands, out nearly to Midway and Johnston Islands and across French Frigate Shoals, to end up close to Molokai as maneuvers ended. Naturally, it is around these waters that sooner or later in an actual engagement we may have to meet the enemy. It is because of the vital importance of the Hawaiian Islands that we spent so much time practicing how to defend them. By six thirty the battle line was streaming past that leper colony for which Molokai is noted, skirting the smaller island of Lanai to the south.

"Great balls of fire," Beany said, as the wind shrieked down the Venturi-like channel between Molokai and Maui, "grab me, or I'll go swimmin' with the natives!"

He wasn't fooling. There is a peculiar channel between Maui and Molokai, through which there is nearly always a strong, steady wind of about 25 knots velocity. He held onto a wing of one of the planes, all of which had been securely lashed down to the deck. The strong wind bustled across the flight deck, banging the loose control surfaces and rustling across the taut fabric wings. We all hung on like Beany. When the ship had rounded the sheltered side of Maui to swing into her berth, we were all sitting down along the edge of the flight deck, feet dangling in the guard net, to watch a typical Hawaiian sunset sink down behind Lanai. To most of us this was all new scenery, and we couldn't have been as excited about the whole thing if we had been aboard the Astor yacht.

There are eight islands in the Hawaiian group that form a hub for United States strategy in the Pacific. All of them lie somewhat close together except Kauai and Niihau, which are perhaps eighty miles from the main island of Oahu. Molokai, Lanai, Maui, and Kahoolawe form a closed array of sea mountains centered between Oahu and Hawaii, and only about eight or ten miles of blue water separates them. Once you have seen the greenness of the foliage on these verdant hills, the warm, peaceful breeze bending the cane rows behind lazy-looking white verandas and rambling houses, the stalk-thatched roofs of the native huts, you begin to wonder how such a peaceful spot could be one of the strongest naval bases in the world. Yet it is.

That evening, while the two destroyers mothered close by to get their supply of fuel, McClure, a veteran of Pacific cruises, told us what we would find at Honolulu on the island of Oahu. Nuessle, Vensel, Ottinger, and I sat around on the flight deck in the cool evening breeze, watching the big yellow Hawaiian moon glitter across the water. I can see why people go out to Hawaii to live. They must all be perpetually in the throes of spring fever. As Mac gave us the dope, the past weeks of howling engines, racing propellers, screaming dives, and grueling formation flying seemed years back.

"Oahu," Mac said, "is the chief fortified island in the group. We'll anchor just above Diamond Head, almost directly out from Waikiki Beach, and you'll be able to see the surfboarders from the deck. Pearl Harbor, our patrol-plane base, will be jammed with destroyers and submarines even before we get there, and you'll see about twice as many PBY's [Consolidated patrol bombers] as we have at San Diego. Remember the four big boats that flew up alongside the squadron when we were out to get the *Idaho* and *Tennessee?* They were from Pearl Harbor."

Mac counted off the numerous Army forts on his fingers. "There's Fort Ruger, Derussy, Armstrong, Shafter, Barrette, and Weaver, all located along the edge of the island from Diamond Head to Pearl Harbor. The Army's main hangout is called Schofield Barracks, which is just above Wheeler Field, where they do most of their flying. The island is more like a gun turret with foliage and trees for camouflage than a vacation spot."

Then he told us what to see and how to see it— and how much *okulihow* to drink at one sitting. You soon realize on an air base how pleasant it is to have the "old-timers" around. They give you plenty of good, useful information, and you soon learn to respect them, knowing that what they put out has been bought only through experience. Below again, I found a long letter from Bud that the mail plane had brought to La Haina the day before. One of our motor whaleboats had gone ashore and hauled the pouches back to the ship. After nearly a month without any personal news from home, you get a lot of respect for the mail planes. There was some news about the air station back at North Island and what was happening, and after Beany settled down to read a "manuscript" from his "friend," as he called her, I got the dope from Bud.

" . . . Don Avrill, the little yellow-haired second looie that you played cribbage with the last time you were up at the squadron ready room, crashed up in the mountains near Falbrook yesterday. He and Mike were climbing to thirty thousand feet to test machine guns for cold-weather operation, when, according to Mike, who was following, Don's plane pulled up in a lazy loop and started down in a dive. Mike followed him down, pouring on the coal to stay with him, but said he hit four hundred fifty, with Avrill still beating him to the ground, and at two thousand feet Mike pulled out. All we can figure is that Don's oxygen failed when he got to thirty thousand, and he just never did wake up.

"When the plane—one of our new Grummans—hit, there was a hell of a fire. Plane exploded and started burning the underbrush up the side of the mountain. It was a pretty nasty mess, and they didn't get much of Don to send home. All we could find of the plane was about half of the rudder. That was the first bad crack-up we've had in the outfit, and the boys are pretty much down on medical research in general for not figuring out a more positive source of oxygen supply than this 'pipe-stem' hookup the Navy is using. You know, all a guy needs at thirty thousand feet is to let that little stem slip out of his mouth for a couple of seconds, and his number is up for keeps.

"The base is really quiet. Our squadron, a utility group, and one patrol outfit who are getting ready to fly nonstop out to Pearl Harbor are the only units left. I had two cross-country's—one to San Francisco and one out to Las Vegas and Boulder Dam. I gotta admit that excitement is lacking here, and we'll be glad to see you flying gobs pull in next month. How is the war going, and where is my brown-skinned gal? Last dispatch we had here on your maneuvers said that the *Ranger* was keeping your faces red and stealing the show! Keep your wings on, and I'll see you when the cruise is over.

"Like the handle on a soup plate.

"Bud"

Like many of the other boys on their first big cruise, I got just a slight touch of nostalgia from reading about home goings on, even if we did have several days of sightseeing around Honolulu. Of course, the first big scramble, as always, when the fleet gets into Honolulu, was up to the Alexander Young Hotel to blow off a little steam and see all the boys from the other units of the fleet. You can't blame them for that. Weeks at sea, cooped up on a floating landing field, flying long hours over blank water, seeing the same faces at the same place each day, listening (I believe, even in your sleep) for "man all flight quarter stations" or "man all battle stations," crawling out early in the morning to deafen your ears behind a roaring engine while you strained for some sign of the enemy were definite reason for a little relaxation.

And Honolulu knew it! Signs of welcome were plastered on every store and in every show window. "Welcome, Navy." "Hello, gobs—have fun." The one that got me was in a Chinese gift shop. It read, "Last time you wrecked store but allee samee—welcome back Uncle Samee." (That smart Chinese had probably graduated from Yale or Princeton. He got the business.)

Small deviations from the town rules and regulations were quietly overlooked. We scampered down to famous Waikiki for a swim and out to the Royal

Hawaiian to the welcoming dance that evening. It was a bit stuffy to us, what with all the gold braid in full dress, dancing stiffly around the glazed floor with "their ladies." I cornered "Bushy" Bushman, black-haired, solemn sort of fellow who finished at Pensacola with me. Bushy had been sent out to Pearl Harbor with Patrol Squadron Ten the day he got his wings, and he had been here ever since.

"How do you like living here on the island?" I said. "Don't you get an awful itch to get back to some of Louis Armstrong's dirty swing music, see some good old American football or baseball games, and take a little trip home to see the folks?"

I could feel his answer before he said it. Nearly every man I talked with out there who had been sent out on duty liked it for keeps. They seemed to be completely content to spend the rest of their days in Honolulu, if it was possible.

"It's really swell," said Bushy. "Here we start to the squadron early, about six, and finish up at two or two thirty most afternoons. That gives us the whole long afternoon to spend at the beach, on the golf course, or sailing around the island in the Star boats the base has. I wouldn't trade it for anything, and if I can I am going to try to get a job flying for Inter-Island when my tour of duty is over."

I thought maybe he was kidding about not wanting to get back to the mainland. I found that he wasn't.

"I guess life is pretty easy here, even though we do fly a lot. My section has been out on patrol duty for the last three weeks straight. We take off about seven in the morning and stay up in a sector between here and Hawaii straight on through until two. A couple of times we have flown a stretch of eighteen hours, taking our coffee mess and lunch pails with us. It isn't all roses."

Bushman was as brown as the natives who were pushing their outriggers into the surf for an evening of riding the crests. A lot of the people stood around the promenade railing, watching the sight you usually see in the movies.

"I'd like to go home about once a year, just to keep in touch with things, but after that—give me the life of an islander!"

That was nearly three years ago. Bushy wasn't fooling. He is still there, from the last report, and quite a few more of the boys are, also. Pearl Harbor seems to be one base that Uncle Sam doesn't have to try very hard to sell to his aviators. Next day we strolled through the cluttered streets along the waterfront, amused at the conglomeration of races present, which included Caucasians, Polynesians, Chinese, Japanese, and an intermingling that had us stopped. Everyone had something to sell to the American sailor boys, and they were putting on the high pressure before the fleet pulled out. Over at the seaplane and patrol base at Pearl Harbor we spent the better part of two days visiting with classmates who had been sent there for duty, listening to their stories of the islands, who had cracked up, how they enjoyed working from six until two, with the lazy afternoons free to swim on the beach or partake of such strenuous games as tennis and handball. Already the talk was going around about what each fellow was going to do after his tour of duty was up. We heard the usual spiel about the Japanese fishing boats, which were presumed to follow our fleet when the maneuvers were on and get valuable information on our tactical dispositions. (In all the cruises I made in the Navy, I have yet to see the sampans that caused all the talk, though there were many references during operations to sampans and small fishing boats' being seen in the vicinity of the fleet.)

Down on the big concrete ramps in front of the hangars along the beach were the big boat-patrol outfits, the ones that only five days before we had "bombed" out on French Frigate Shoals. These big flying barns are worth talking about, for they are going to play an important part in any warfare the Navy gets tangled with. Nearly all our present patrol planes are built by Consolidated Aircraft Corporation. There are squadrons of them located at San Diego, Coco Solo, Sitka, Norfolk, and now they stretch out to the new and far-flung bases at Wake Island, Midway, Samoa, Guam, and the score of newest proposed air bases around the South Pacific.

Performance of these huge "flying bomb racks" is more than gratifying. It is reassuring. With a crew of from six to eleven, a cruising range of some several thousand miles, and plenty of striking power in bombs and machine guns, these giants can live in the air for twenty-five or thirty hours and perform miracles as the eyes of the scouting force. Many times during the cruise we had seen them flying far at sea, day and night, keeping their lonely vigil in a wide radius about our battle line, sounding off the alarm by radio when an attack was imminent.

Here, at their base at Pearl Harbor, they were being scrubbed down and checked, being made ready to go again. Replacements are simply flown the twenty-four hundred miles across the ocean from San Diego. I know of three such mass flights, which included twenty patrol bombers on each one, and not once was one of them lost or even forced down at sea on the way across. In time of actual warfare these flying battleships, with their stately manner, will be invaluable to the scouting force of the Navy, and their striking power is a reassuring threat to any would-be invader by air or sea.

I remember the difference in these long rows of patrol planes, proved and worthy, which lined the ramp at Pearl Harbor and the small scattering of big boats I saw at Brest just before the capitulation of France. The naval base at Brest was the pride of a faltering French Navy, and the woefully few inadequate seaplanes there made me actually feel sorry for the Frenchmen. The nine *hydravion de surveillance maritime* that were concentrated on

Plougastel, the point of land across the bay from the fleet base at Brest, were composed of old Loire 130's, several antique Cams 37's, all wire and braces, and a few Brequets and Latecoere 302's. These were powered by troublesome Hispanos of old and vulnerable design, and even though the sea warfare at that time was intense through the channel the Frenchmen never could seem to get these outmoded machines into the air for any length of time. When one of these lumbering Brequets actually sank a German submarine off the Île d'Ouessant one day early in January, 1940, the crew of six were feted all the way to Paris and back. I thought then how I would have liked to play Santa Claus to them and set a few squadrons of our sleek, high-performing bombers down in front of their lonely ramp.

The last night before we shoved off for San Francisco, Vensel, Garrison, Ewers, and I climbed up to the top of the Punchbowl to watch the twinkling lights of Honolulu and the flashing streaks from the fleet's searchlights as they played through the night, making an aerial display for the townfolk. It was sort of a going-away gesture of *aloha* from the fleet to the natives of the island for a pleasant shore leave in their port. You can imagine how sad the store and shop proprietors were to see us pull out next day, leaving them to sell their souvenirs to the current tourists. It must have seemed very dead in the city with the noise of Navy gobs on shore leave gone and the thousands of white uniforms that crowded every sidewalk suddenly missing.

In one of the gift shops, I found a brown-skinned, native hula dancer, with grass skirt and all. I purchased it from the jabbering Chinese and stowed it safely in my trunk. Basil Alexander Martin, Jr., could never say I didn't bring him what he asked for from the land of poi and pineapple!

Next morning we weighed anchor, followed the big, squatty battleship, the *California*, out of the Roads, rounded Diamond Head, and lay a course out across the ocean for San Francisco. Our two plane-guard destroyers trailed along behind and were followed in cruising disposition by the carriers *Saratoga*, *Ranger*, and *Enterprise*. We finally had got together with the *Ranger!*

Chapter XI

In case you are not familiar with the various types of planes that fly from an aircraft-carrier deck, their purpose, and the various formations they assume in performing their missions, a brief review might be interesting.

Each carrier, as a unit, is composed of one fighting squadron, one scouting squadron, one light-bombing or dive-bombing squadron, and one heavy-bombing and torpedo squadron. The fighters are a squadron of single-seater airplanes that are aboard the carrier for just one purpose—fighting. Fast, highly maneuverable, bulging with guns, these stubby hornets form the protective patrol high above the ship and can accompany bombers on their missions to ward off enemy attackers. The scouts are two-seater airplanes, with long-range cruising capabilities, and it is up to them to scout for the enemy fleet, report positions and courses, and even attack with relatively light bombs to supplement the heavy bombers. The dive bombers are also two-place planes, carrying an ample supply of medium-heavy bombs, and are used for diving attacks on enemy cruisers, battleships, carriers, and shore bases. Dive bombers are becoming faster and faster as the speed of the fighting planes increases in order to reach their objective and return without too great a loss of pilots and equipment en route. Last come the torpedo or heavy bombers, three-place, somewhat slower planes that usually receive the escort protection of the fighters as they seek out their objective and either torpedo or heavily bomb it with devastating results.

After the squadrons are rendezvoused off the deck and have set out for their objectives, they usually assume a spread-out formation in which the individual planes fly wider spread so as to make it less tiresome for the pilots. This may be a formation in which the sections (three planes) fly in wide V's or one in which they fly in echelon. (An echelon is a formation in which the planes are "stacked up," so to speak, on one side of the leader, each plane being slightly off to the side, slightly to the rear, and a little above the plane below.)

In most maneuvers in the fleet one of these two formations is used, for they provide an elastic method of maneuvering airplanes as a body. The individual sections assume these positions in the divisions and likewise the divisions in the squadron, so that the fundamental or basic formations of individual planes hold true also for sections, divisions, squadrons, and even wings. In all cases the planes maintain a "stepped-up" position while cruising about the sky, so that if you are flying near the tail end of a squadron in formation you actually look down the line of planes to the leader instead of straight ahead, as it appears from the ground. The main reason for the "stepped-up" flying is to keep out of the various slip streams of the planes ahead; but also it is easier for the pilots to see signals from the planes below.

Naturally, for special occasions, various other formations are used. This holds true, for instance, in flying parades or performing unorthodox maneuvers for an air show or air meet. In these formations the individual planes are tucked in close to the plane ahead, so that the pilot is deadly alert to the slightest change of speed or position by his leader. There is a constant growling of gunned engines and blatting props as each man works his throttle and jockeys for position in close to the next plane. The slightest movement of the controls by the leader must be anticipated by the pilots behind when flying a "tight" formation, for danger of collision is always imminent.

Many a time you will find your heart in your throat as you glance down into the cockpit for a quick look at your instruments and look up to find your wing almost into the tail of the plane ahead. In flying a "close formation" there is little time to look anywhere except straight at the section leader's neck. Anything you want in your own cockpit you get by groping in snatches with one free hand while keeping your eyes open for any movement of the plane ahead.

The day before we arrived outside the Golden Gate Bridge at San Francisco for its dedication our carrier had its last practice parade. It was completed in conjunction with the other carrier groups. All squadron pilots met in the wardroom as usual to get the dope, which the air officer was plotting on a blackboard at one end of the room.

"This, gentlemen," he said, pointing to a squadron of crosses, "is our carrier group. Here are the *Ranger*, the *Enterprise*, and the *Saratoga*. After the squadrons have rendezvoused over their respective carriers, the groups will then rendezvous over the leading battleship, the *New Mexico*, at eight thousand feet. The parade formation will be led back over the entire battle line by the senior group commander, and all group commanders will dress on him. After two passes over the battle line, the break-up signal will be passed, and each squadron commander will take charge, return to the carrier, and wait for the landing order from the ship. All pilots are cautioned to use fuel from their belly tanks first. Run them dry before switching to main, as this flight will necessarily be long and you will need the fuel in the main tank for landing aboard."

Whether I was thinking about the Navy ball at San Francisco the next night or just plain daydreaming I don't know. But that last warning didn't stick with me as we joined up over the carrier and began the process of rendezvousing some three hundred planes for the parade. I watched as Alex signaled us in closer, reveling at the sight of all the shiny planes that were in good clean formation below us. Tomorrow we would be back in the United States. Two days later we should get back to North Island. I looked down the long line of cruisers and plowing battleships that stretched back across the ocean for fifteen miles. My mind was on anything but what was going on in the cockpit. Looking from the back of Nuessle's head across the wing to Vensel for just a glance, I saw him eating an apple. He took a big bite, grinned back at me, and pantomimed that it was excellent—the sawed-off little rascal! He knew I'd be hungry, as usual, about now. The whole four groups of planes from the four carriers were finally rendezvoused, and, led by the senior group commander, we thundered back across the long line of ships below.

"All ships in the air from senior group commander. We will repeat that last parade formation."

I listened to the order come through the earphones but was still thinking about how nice it would be to get back to North Island. Another half hour went by of jockeying the throttle, keeping in position on the section leader, and concentrating on flying a good close formation. Tomorrow we were to show off the pride of the naval air force above the new Golden Gate Bridge. Then I noticed for the first time that I had been flying with my fuel switched to main tank instead of auxiliary. I hastily checked the gauge and switched it over. There was still enough gas in the main tank for landing aboard, but I knew that I didn't have any to waste. (In flying low around a carrier and making a deck landing, the one thing a pilot doesn't want to do is run out of gasoline. The usual practice is to use all the fuel from the auxiliary tank first, so as to have a more accurate fuel-supply check for the more hazardous low flying and landing operation.) Then we got the order to break up and prepare to land back aboard.

It seems that the things that happen to a pilot always happen when he least expects them to or when he has put himself and his plane, through thoughtlessness, in a position in which any unexpected trouble will make the going tough. This was my time to get into such a predicament. When I set the landing-gear switch to the down position to extend the wheels, one wheel didn't come down! As was the general practice, I immediately pulled clear of the landing circle and tried the gear release again. Still no luck. I pulled up clear of the highest of the circling planes. I got to thinking to myself that for the first time in my flying career I was really on the spot. Then I pulled the emergency release to try to lower the wheel that was stuck. A quick glance around told me that there was only about a half hour of daylight remaining, and the sun was already sinking low out in the west behind the last ship in the battle line. The wheel didn't budge. I picked up the microphone.

"*Lexington* from Two Baker Six—my right wheel is stuck and will not release. I have tried the emergency landing-gear release, and it is still up. My position at present is four miles astern of the carrier at five thousand feet. I will try the emergency release again."

The *Lexington* came back hurriedly. "Two Baker Six from *Lexington*—go ahead, but expedite releasing the wheel, as there is a fog drifting over that is expected to be on the water shortly after sundown."

A fine thing. They should tell me to expedite getting that wheel to drop—as if I wasn't hurrying, I thought. Who do they think is sitting up here with a half uncocked landing gear trying to beat the sun down! You always get hot under the collar when you're flying in difficulty and some dodo on the ground or ship leans back in his chair and starts telling you the situation is getting serious. Anyway, the clean, free air is a good place to give vent to your feelings.

Then the main tank ran dry. One cough and a dying sputter, and the engine quit. My heart almost quit with it! I shifted to belly tank and grabbed the wobble pump. It caught again and ran smoothly, but I knew now that from here on it was no fun. There was no way of telling how much fuel was left in that auxiliary tank! It was just pray that the supply held out.

Behind me in the rear cockpit sat Larue, a big, sturdy mechanic, first class. Larue had been flying with me from the first day I hit the fleet, except the time I landed on the side of the mountain at San Clements. He had been on leave that day. Now he was in for a crash landing that didn't look so easy! As I peered back past the life raft he grinned, crossed his fingers, and shook his hand. Good old Larue. Just a big smile all over his face. A tap on his earphones showed me as he nodded that he had listened to the conversation. I forced a grin back at him, thinking, there is the type of man the Navy wants. How damned reassuring it was to have someone with that make-up along in this mess. A quick check on the indicator showed the right wheel still stuck up in its hatbox.

By this time all other planes were aboard, and the sun was well down into the horizon, dulled by the fog that was moving over the ship. I had visions of the rest of the boys down in the wardroom, getting ready for dinner, all safely down and secure. It's funny how you think in terms of comfort and security that is so close after you get into an unexpected jam. You remember all the times that everything had gone off as routine in your landings—so routine that you have never given a thought to a situation like this!

If only there was enough fuel in that tank! Damn! but it was uncomfortable to sit there and not know when you might run out of gas. Below, the carrier rolled and pitched more regularly as she picked up speed, sending white spray off her bow like sudden flares. The two knifing cans were trailing behind, splitting the eerie-looking wake that penciled an almost blackened sea.

"*Lexington* from Two Baker Six—I cannot get

(*Official Photograph, U. S. Navy.*)

A division of Grumman shipboard fighters in attack formation—the "protective patrol."

the gear down. Right wheel stuck hard in the hatbox, and emergency is no good. I am running low on gasoline and will have to land soon."

The sound of my own voice in the microphone was strange, though I tried to sound matter of fact. Funny how you can get self-conscious at such a time, especially after reading stories about all the guys that kept cool in pickles such as this was turning out to be. I dropped down lower to keep the carrier in sight and suddenly thought of the last resort, the last chance to free that wheel. Why hadn't that occurred to me before?

"*Lexington*, I am going to cut the line to the switch and attempt to release the hydraulic pressure."

The ship answered in short, terse sentences. "O.K., Guyton. Watch your gas. If the gear doesn't release drop your belly tank and come aboard. We are going to give you all the wind we can over the deck."

I slid my hand along the side of the fuselage, unsheathed the small saw that was part of the emergency equipment in all planes, and began sawing the line. It was better not to think about the gas now. I passed close abeam the ship, only a few hundred feet up. The deck was a mass of yellow lights, and the faces of hundreds of men stared up at us as we crossed the stern. I began to think about the *Lexington's* order to drop the belly tank. I couldn't do that, or we wouldn't have any gas at all! I told the ship about it, but they didn't answer, and I could imagine the captain pacing the bridge muttering, "Young fool—damned young fool!"

Landing with the belly tank on was a real fire hazard, and I knew it. But the mistake caused by my earlier carelessness couldn't be corrected now. The line was almost in two. There! Seven hundred pounds of pressure sent a small geyser of hydraulic fluid all over the cockpit. The half castor oil and half wood alcohol hit me in the face and covered the windshield. Half choking for breath, I tore the slimy helmet and goggles away and leaned out into the slip stream for a breath of something besides those sickening fumes. Behind me Larue was doing the same.

"*Lexington* from . . . " The oily microphone slipped from my hands and went down on the floor. I grabbed for it, and for a second the ship and its lighted deck disappeared from view. My heart stood at rigid attention as I thought of hitting that black void—somewhere on the Pacific Ocean! Somehow I ducked again into the cockpit and groped for the mike. The ship was calling.

"Guyton, come on in and land. You can't have much gas left, and the fog is getting thick!" I knew they were right, for the ghostly fog clouds were making even the blackness of the ocean below disappear. I'd have to land on one wheel.

"O.K., *Lexington*." I found the mike, at the same time spotting through the blowing mist the rows of lights along the gunwales, which now looked like heaven itself after having disappeared for a few seconds. I thought of Larue but just for a second. That kind of man would sit there and take anything—a real Navy iron man. I swung around the stern low, offered a silent prayer that the gas wouldn't give out, and crossed into the groove ahead of the first rolling destroyer. The clouded windshield was out of the question, so with one eye out in the slip stream I hung on the wands, riding in on Sperry's signals. It happened fast. The stern flashed by, the lighted wand waved, made the "cut." I jerked back on the throttle, threw the switch off, and ducked.

There was a scraping crunch and a hard jolt that

rocked my nose against the gun sight. The plane slithered around to the right, bounced up on its nose, and tilted on the propeller hub. Then the tail came down with a hard slap, and the engine stopped in a shower of sparks. The deck handling crew were all around us as I felt myself crawling over the side behind Larue, wondering if either of us was hurt and why that belly tank hadn't exploded. Then the daze cleared away, and the crash detail, the asbestos man, and a doctor rushed up.

The doc yelled over to the stretcher carriers. "No work tonight, boys," he said, waving Larue away. As he uncrossed my fingers I began to feel the swelling in my face.

"A broken nose and one split lip, young fellow," the doc said, walking me over beneath the gun turret, away from the crowd. "We'll have you fixed up in no time."

I think the doc was just a bit excited after the long ordeal of "waiting" for a sure patient. Larue wasn't hurt at all. He had taken the gas cap off and was tapping the tank with a stick. Then he caught up with us. "About two gallons left, sir," he said with a grin.

That fixed up my part of the dedication parade

and the Navy ball that followed next day at San Francisco. In fact, I didn't get ashore at all. Imagine sitting in your bunk listening to the squadron take off to do some fancy formation flying over the good old United States! Imagine sitting there listening to a radio that night as the announcer went on and on about the gala affairs happening in town! The big dress ball took place at the Fairmont up on Nob Hill, but the whole afternoon was open house at any hotel in town. The boys told me about it that night.

"Great day in the morning, Guy," Beany said. "There we were, trying to pay the taxi driver, and the big lug wouldn't take a cent, not one cent. Said it was on the city! Never heard of such a thing before."

"Yeah," Bunky Ottinger put in. "I had three dinners at three different hotels, and that didn't include the hors d'oeuvres at the Palace in the afternoon! They said our money wasn't any good and to just help ourselves." (Bunky could eat more than two ordinary men. He wasn't any bigger than a fair-sized minute, but none of us could ever understand why. His calories per day must run to a figure like the national debt!)

The parade had been a huge success, and the papers came out with beautiful colored pictures of the whole three hundred and thirty airplanes flying a closed formation over the new span. The Chamber of Commerce had met weeks before and decided that the city would be turned over to the Navy for the afternoon and evening. They did just that, too, and many of Uncle Sammy's boys in blue have fond memories of the festive spirit that spilled over into the famous San Francisco fog that night. Now that the war is threatening and all personnel and equipment of the Navy are bent on just one purpose—preparation—these affairs belong to the good old days.

It was only a year later that half the fleet sailed down through the Panama Canal, across to Cuba, and up the East Coast to New York as a sort of test move to prove the efficient transfer, via the canal, of the Pacific fleet. Here the situation was much the same. Banquets, parties, and dances were set up for the roster of Uncle Sam's Navy, and it made you just a little proud to be a member of an organization that was so well thought of and appreciated.

I couldn't go ashore for the big blowout at San

Francisco, but I didn't miss the President's inspection the next morning. During the night sometime, I heard the rattle and rumble as the anchor went down, and when we got up on deck about nine o'clock the ship stood to, facing the long rows of docks off Market Street. It was a very colorful affair. Nearly every ship of the Pacific fleet lay at anchor in San Francisco Bay, all in full dress, scrubbed spotless, with brasswork shining and sparkling in the bright sun. On deck, with the planes all pushed nearly back along the sides and stowed below on the hangar deck, we stood at attention, ready to "man the rail" when the President passed by in the Admiral's barge.

Our total crew of nearly two thousand officers and men, dressed in white uniforms, lined the full length of the flight deck in four even lines. Off in the lower part of the bay you could hear the twenty-one-gun salute fired by one of the battleships, and from another part, shortly after, the national anthem floated softly across the water. As the President and his party passed close by the starboard side and our own band struck up, I kept wondering if they were coming aboard or if they picked only on the battle-force flagship, the *California*, for actual ship inspection.

As I stared out across the water at the *Pennsylvania*, one of the first "big five" of our entire fleet, I felt not storybook pride but a feeling of satisfaction. The feeling had struck me the day our war games had ended, the day the commander in chief of the Pacific fleet had sent out his dispatch to all ships. It read, "Congratulations all units Pacific fleet. It was a job well done." That was all. But after those weeks of honest sweat, when some forty-five thousand men manned forty-five thousand battle stations, each doing his job, whether it was commanding a battleship, peeking through a conning tower, flying a plane, or scrubbing a deck—after being a part of this tremendous team I couldn't help but get a slight stiffening of the spine. I think every other man did, too, as he stood there reminiscing over the past weeks about the "job well done." And as I stood there watching the full-dress flags of the *Pennsy* wave back along the sea breeze, I thought about what a naval officer had once told me.

"There is something about the Navy that is unexplainable, and you who weren't raised on its traditions will probably think it a bit on the dramatic side," he said. "But as you go along day to day, doing your job to the best of your ability, trying not to let someone else carry the load for you, that 'something' grows. Maybe it is serving your country that gives you the pride you feel. I'm not sure. All I can tell you is that no matter how hard or naïve the sailor or officer appears in the naval service, if he is doing his job well, he feels it inside—and he's proud."

I knew what he meant now. When we first came into the Navy I thought about the sport of flying, the pleasure of travel, the bonus that Uncle Sam was offering, the clean living that was ahead. It had just looked like a good job. I didn't know anything about "serving your country," "doing your bit," "carrying on." They were meaningless terms as I went to draw my pay check.

Now, after two years, standing here on the deck of a ship I had served with alongside two thousand other shipmates, I felt that something. You may think it's funny—or that it smacks of Hollywood. I don't. And I started from scratch, a farm boy from Missouri, who had never seen a battleship or destroyer or heard the phrase "carry on!"

AIR BASE

I came to again as the word was passed to man the rail. We all about-faced and stepped to the sides of the flight deck as the barge went by. We came to a salute as one, and then our part of the ceremony was over. I was glad to take my bandaged head down into the cool of the wardroom and relax. Standing at attention in a broiling sun, wearing a full-dress uniform, sword and all, is not the most relaxing way to spend two hours. You get your fill of parades before you even leave Pensacola, but by the time you have stood three or four captain's inspections with your squadron on the air base, you have learned to relax somewhat, though standing at attention.

I remember one time when we were standing an inspection on the white ramp in front of the hangar at Pensacola's Squadron Four. It was one hundred and one degrees in a Florida sun, and forty-four cadets stood at parade rest and then at attention for one long, immeasurable hour. The man next to me turned gray, then white and sickly looking. He tottered slightly and, before anyone could catch him, fell full forward on his face. I don't know why it didn't hurt him, because that concrete was just as hard as it was hot. But he was carried off into the shade to revive, and after an hour or so was O.K. He had started something, though, and we began to think being overcome by the heat was contagious. Before the inspection was over seven more had followed him, and it gave you the impression—if you let your imagination roam—that someone out in the bay you were facing had a machine gun and was getting his share!

Not that this meant that the brass hats in the Navy were just a bunch of old meanies. They know all about such things as inspections and what goes with them. If you just remember that they went through the same thing before they acquired all the stripes and that there are tricks to such necessary proceedings that make them easy, you'll soon cool off and not feel hurt about the whole thing.

The next morning at three the *Lexington* weighed anchor and trailed along out of the bay in the long file of gray warships to head for San Diego. Alex stopped by the room that morning after breakfast as Beany and I were packing our clothes. "How do you feel?" he asked. I told him I felt O.K. except for the soreness in my nose. He sat around for a while, talking about the cruise and the gunnery exercises we had coming up after leave period was over. He started out the door and then turned around again.

"Oh, yes," he said, "you are going to fly ashore in Vensel's back seat. His mechanic will stay aboard the ship and stand by the two wrecked airplanes."

Then he went out. That was just like old Alex, and you find that kind of camaraderie almost anywhere in the Navy. Alex knew what it meant to fly ashore from your first big cruise instead of waiting for several hours and then going in by launch or motorboat. Naturally, I couldn't fly my own plane, which was minus a propeller and a wing from the crack-up, but he had arranged it so I wouldn't miss a big moment of this first cruise, and I was duly thankful.

"What were you born with, a platinum spoon in your mouth?" Beany said after Alex had gone. "I had visions of you going ashore on the barge with your cracked-up space wagon sometime tomorrow night. Some stuff!" Beany threw a pair of socks in a laundry bag. "Say," he said, turning around suddenly with a funny look on his face. "I'm gonna' go home on leave and get married!"

I almost dropped a whole suitcase. Ever since I

first met Vensel, he had paid no more attention to women than to the size of his opponent when he wanted a scrap. Now, out of a clear blue sky, after saying not one word in the months I had been living with him, he wanted his leave period to go home and get married! A lot of funny things can happen in the service.

I remembered all the nights we had lain awake in our bunks during the cruise, the ship blacked out, with nothing to do but talk yourself to sleep. We had discussed the peculiar circumstances that brought us into Navy flying in the first place, what we had started out to be in life, why we didn't do it, what we wanted to do after our tour of duty was over in a couple of years, and just about everything else in general. And all the time Beany had a secret he never spilled! Even his "manuscript to a friend" hadn't given me a clue!

The next morning, as we climbed to join the squadron and headed for Point Loma, sticking out in the distance, I enjoyed a free ride, sitting comfortably cocked back in the gunner's seat in the rear cockpit. My nose had settled back on my face. Alex lead us around the point, over the lighthouse, and out across the strand below Coronado.

We made a wide sweep, closed up in a tight formation, and roared back low over North Island. We were back home! I can't forget the difference between flying ashore from a big cruise before war had started and what takes place when the squadrons come back now.

As we flew over the island, you could see the officers and enlisted men's families standing out along the edge of the mat, waving and watching. We spread out in a big V formation, slid back into sections, and turned back across the field to break up into three-plane groups and get down into the landing circle when our turn came. Those cars down there that lined the roads to the air station were full of families waiting for "daddy" to come home. Along the docks where the destroyers and cruisers would send their launches and motorboats ashore were more crowds that had a longer wait. The ships had just begun to file into San Diego Bay. Above us, as we dropped down into the landing lane, were the squadrons from the other carriers that would follow with the same parade "salute" to the folks on the ground.

It was quite an impressive home-coming. Now, ship movements, departures and arrivals, fleet operations, and maneuvers are all completed with the least noticeable disturbance. Even the families of the personnel aboard remain, necessarily, in complete ignorance of the whereabouts, departures, or arrivals of units of the fleet. At the present time the officers based with the Atlantic fleet on the East Coast don't know where the Pacific fleet is and vice versa.

We landed on the mat with a bounce and a squeal of brakes, and I chided Beany through the interphone as we taxied up to the line. It's a famous practice in service flying. When a brother pilot is a passenger in your back seat you had better put on a good performance, or you're in for some good friendly teasing, which is no more than mocking the instructor's "hair tearing" you used to cause in Pensacola as a dodo bird.

Even before the wheels were against the chocks, I could see Basil Alexander Martin, Jr., standing on the running board of "Hotdamn." I got my share of razzing as soon as the big leatherneck saw the tape on my nose.

"Well, sailor boy," he said, "it sure looks like this wasn't a play war you all went on. Machine gun or shrapnel?"

I told him that I had had a little accident, knowing full well that one Lieutenant Martin would never be satisfied until he had the whole story. We jumped into "Hotdamn" and made our way through the crowds that were watching the last squadron of the *Enterprise* as they circled overhead and began to break up for a landing. It wasn't too hard to get down to the flying field around the hangars before war had started, even though this was fully restricted and patrolled—that is, for a special occasion such as the fleet's coming home.

You can imagine any guard trying to hold a bunch of Navy wives who were trying to see their husbands for the first time in three or four months! That is why we had the crowds right down in front of the hangars on the edge of the field. But when the United States Navy began to perform its continuous maneuvers and practices after total national defense went to work, it was worth your life to get past even the guards at the outer gates. Many times lately I have had the extreme displeasure of meeting the efficient guard on duty at the naval air station at Anacostia, D.C., one of the Navy's biggest aviation test and supply bases.

(*Official Photograph, U. S. Navy.*)

The aircraft carrier *Lexington* weighs anchor and trails along out to sea with the fleet.

"Do you have any identification, sir?" the sentry asks. I proceed to bring out my naval aviator's designation, my ring from Pensacola graduation, and several papers denoting my urgent business with the commanding officer.

"Sorry, sir," the sentry says very politely. "I'll have an escort for you in a few minutes, and then you can proceed."

That is how strict the government must be in time of war or national emergency. Not only that, but your "escort," a marine with side arms all ready for business, will stick right with you until you are definitely recognized and taken in charge by the officer you are seeking.

By the time the home-coming party got under way at the officers' club that night, I was practically talked out explaining to Bud just what went on during the cruise, what Hawaii was like, and how I happened to miss the big blowout at San Francisco.

We found the officers' club all decked out in its finest reception form, and even the orchestra off in the corner was wearing evening dress to make the affair completely formal. It had started to be the usual costume Hawaiian dress ball at first, but someone had decided that times were a little too questionable, with all the war talk going on, so the entertainment committee posted their "dress tonight" sign. We found a table and sat down and carried on while most of the boys blew off a little steam on the dance floor or gathered in larger bull sessions. It was interesting just to "sit there and listen."

"Boy, what a squadron I belong to," one of the young fellows was saying. "We almost beat the 'Hotshots' landing-interval record of last year. Didn't have but two crack-ups, either."

I noticed that the speaker was one of the boys who formerly had said to me in the utmost confidence, "I sure don't go in for this hangar flying or shooting the breeze about a guy's squadron. Can't see the percentage. We're out here to fly, earn some dough, and get a bonus in the end, without getting 'rah rah' about it. If we do our job O.K. and Uncle Sam is satisfied, I can't see that we have to get so all-fired interested in the general welfare of our squadron organization. After all, we have only three years to be in the Navy!"

He had definitely been one of the reserved, aloof types and had started out at North Island by spending the evening sessions unenthusiastically discussing what went on during the day in his squadron or how he "shot a target full of holes" or what he found was the best method of sinking a bomb in the center of a circle while diving upwind. I sat listening, and so did Martin.

"And talk about a swell skipper," the chap went on. "When we got to Honolulu he gave all of the junior officers the first night ashore and had the older boys volunteer for the watches aboard ship. Everyone of us piled into the eight o'clock shore boat, and the skipper came along. When we got to the Alexander Young, he asked us all up to join his party on the roof garden!"

Now that this formerly "unmoved by Navy traditions" gentleman had made his first cruise, had associated closely with his brother fliers, and had been scratched by this "something" in naval tradition that I spoke about before, he was becoming just as enthusiastic about his part of the "blue and gold" as I had.

It's like a high school star entering college with the declaration that he "will never go out for the football team" because he is there to study. Then he accidentally moseys down by the athletic field, sees the pigskin rocket through the air, hears the voices of the coming team as they plan their season, and—kerplop! Before the young would-be refrainer figures it out he is right in the thick of the game. Maybe I'm a wishful, romantic sort of guy. I never did need any urging to feel just a little proud that I was in the service of my country. And despite all the decrying and tabooing about the romance of flying in this day and age, you can still get a kick out of landing a snarling fighter in front of a crowd of gaping, staring laymen, with a nonchalance that is not all natural.

We were just getting warmed to a discussion of the good and bad of Navy flying when Lieutenant Ben Scott pulled up a chair and joined us. "You'll have to count me in on this session, you young upstarts," Ben said, as the majority of Uncle Sam's fleet air detachment entertained themselves around us. Ben was not exactly a philosopher, but he did a lot of good constructive thinking—and he had flown a lot with the Navy. We had bumped into him when we first arrived in the fleet at one of the squadron parties and were indebted to him for many a "tip" on what to do and what not to do aboard the base. On the cruise it had taken only about six thousand lessons and several cases of Coca-Cola for Ben to teach me that I wasn't any champion at the Navy's own game of "ace-duecey!" Ben was a flier in Scouting Two.

As we sat around the table talking a little about flying and a little about the war situation, the discussion got around to how much *esprit de corps* the flying squadrons had had in the last war and how we didn't think that the squadrons today were all out for that "all for one and one for all" spirit that had flown over the front lines in those days. Ben leaned over to outclass the noise and proceeded to spill a very important mouthful of ideas that I have never forgotten.

"You know," he said, "I was just reading about the flying squadrons of the war back in 1918, and I've figured out why they had so much fighting spirit in those outfits. It's in the name! Richthofen's Flying Circus, the Lafayette Escadrille! Who doesn't remember those two squadrons and the tales of heroism that followed them down to the present day?" Ben lighted a cigarette and went on. I could already sense that he had a good point.

"You know how proud the pilots of those outfits were and how hard the boys who went over tried to get into the Lafayette Escadrille. We ought to have more of that stuff in our flying services. Take Guy here, for instance. He belongs to the 'High Hat' squadron, as hard-flying a bombing squadron as ever took up the game. Do you think he doesn't feel a little *esprit de corps* toward that bunch of 'nothing but the best' fliers who go out to do their work as the much-noticed 'High Hatters'? And how about the 'Hotshots,' a fighting squadron you heard about while still in Pensacola, worrying an instructor."

Yes, I could see Ben had a point. Somehow, though the days of the helmeted hero flying the Spad at a flock of Huns is past, the fighting pilot, I am sure, still feels that tiny tingle of romance as he opens up his throttle and roars out of a field with his squadron. I still do. After seven years of bombing, carrier flying, test flying, air-line flying, I still feel just a trace of the flag-waving crowd and the cheers or looks of awe as I land at an airport. Every pilot must feel it to some extent, because it's natural.

"I think we ought to get some names for our squadrons today and get away from these numbers we have," Ben said. "I can't see where there is anything impractical about instilling a little of the romantic spirit into the boys, and you know as well as I that we would all like it." Ben leaned back in his chair. "I sure would like to see that feeling of pride in the individual squadron built up, and I think we might be missing the boat. This business is not the stamped-out robot formation tactics that most people believe it to be. Say what you will, we would still like to be associated with a famous outfit such as the Lafayette Escadrille rather than Scouting Seventy-nine or Bombing Twenty-three."

I've never forgotten Ben Scott's dissertation that evening. It's the sort of thing that you often find in the service, where an officer will do a lot of thinking—the constructive kind—and will want only that it be heard for what it is worth.

Ben left North Island soon after that. He was transferred to a patrol-plane squadron out in Honolulu, and I haven't seen him since. I heard later that he was the pilot who landed alongside a disabled patrol plane far out at sea, with the waves running fifteen feet high. He knew he couldn't get off again and that his plane might go down, but it didn't stop him. I understand that he landed O.K., pulled on board the seven wet and exhausted fliers, and then just sat there with them and waited for assistance from one of the ships. Just before his plane went down, broken by the heavy sea, a light cruiser arrived to pick them up. I wasn't surprised when I heard the report of that rescue. Old Ben Scott is a good example of the type of man the Navy wants for its service, and I am sure he is still carrying on to the best of his ability.

Chapter XII

UNCLE SAM's naval air force does its practice and maneuvers on a well-organized, well-planned schedule. The Navy's fiscal year begins on July 1 and works from there on a four-quarter basis, which is divided so as to permit the maximum of war practice for all units concerned. Usually you find that the summer quarter is given over to leave periods for officers and men and upkeep and overhaul of airplanes.

This includes ferrying old and new planes back and forth across the United States from such points as Norfolk, Virginia, and Anacostia, D. C., where several of the major fleet overhaul bases are located. Naturally, the overhaul of all airplanes cannot be completed at North Island or San Pedro. It is much easier to allow certain types of planes to be flown to the East Coast bases for their overhaul and let the pilots pick up the new planes for replacements to be flown back across the country. In this way a steady stream of airplanes is shuttled back and forth between Anacostia and San Diego, to be placed in what is known as the air battle-force pool, where they await assignment to squadrons needing them.

It is much less expensive for the government to fly the planes back and forth than to ship them by freight, and at the same time naval pilots are made very happy. It is the golden opportunity to go on a nice, long cross-country flight with extra pay allowances. Every pilot who hits the fleet waits for his opportunity to get a "ferry trip." For the first year or so that you are in the fleet chances of getting one are small. Lack of experience is the major factor. When one airplane is cracked up during one of these trips, the saving over the freight charges is nullified for the next thirty or forty planes ferried. But after a year or more, you are expected to have flying sense, and then, when the break comes along, you may be chosen to perform the trip.

One day, shortly after we had returned from the big cruise, Alex called a conference in the ready room. Half the officers were on leave, so there were only twelve of us to carry on the miscellaneous routine work around the squadron until they got back. Our flying consisted of several instrument hops in the old blind flier we had rigged up for practice and a few navigation hops to keep our hand in on the scouting problems. Alex unfolded the dispatch he had in his hand and read us the news.

"It is requested that you nominate one ferry pilot to ferry a Grumman Fighter from Anacostia to San Diego immediately. Assigned officer report to Operations for train ticket to Washington, as there is no plane ready for ferry East." Alex put the paper down. "Who wants to take it?" he asked.

I must have got my hand up first, though I was a little weak with the "I do, captain."

"O.K., Guyton, you're nominated," said Alex, not knowing the thrill I received from his words. "Fighting Six, I understand, needs this replacement as soon as possible for their gunnery exercises coming up the last of next week. If you catch a train tonight you will get to Anacostia by Tuesday, and if the plane is ready, probably shove off from there on Wednesday. That will give you about two days to get back to North Island, so there won't be any time to waste. Tell the yeoman to make up your orders for ferry duty, and get up to Operations with them as soon as you can. You had better get some things packed now."

I had already started for the yeoman's office, all smiles.

"And remember," Alex added, "They want the airplane in a hurry back here—but they want it in good shape. You've been in the squadron long enough to know that it doesn't pay to take chances in any foul flying weather."

I told him I understood, left word with the yeoman to arrange my orders, and rushed out to pack and report for a train ticket at operations office. I wasn't going to fly both ways, but that didn't matter. Here was a trip to Washington to fly one of our fastest single-seater fighters back across those mountains, plains, and rivers that make up the three thousand miles of country. What's more, I was going to do it alone!

It seemed like a week before the train finally pulled into the station at Washington, D. C. Actually, it was only four days.

I read every magazine available and stared out

of the window for hours, wondering how anyone could be content to travel at such a snail's pace after having once flown swiftly through the clean, unrestricted air space overhead. I kept thinking of the joy of flying back alone over all this rugged country we had passed. For the most part the trip was hot, sticky, and dusty, and I was glad to get to my hotel room for a shower and sink down into a big, soft bed before doing anything else. Then, early the next morning, I piled out, grabbed a hasty breakfast, and arrived at the naval air station at Anacostia, nearly out of breath and anxious, like a kid with a new bike, to see my plane.

Inside the door of Operations, amid the general rush and flare of a morning's business at a very busy air station, I finally found my name on the "scheduled out" board.

"May I have your orders, sir?" the yeoman at the desk said. I turned them over to him. "How soon can I check-flight the plane I am to ferry?" I asked. (You always make a short test flight of your airplane to see that everything is O.K. before you shove off on that long grind back to the coast. After all, you sign your life away to get the airplane, three receipts making you responsible for delivery, and it is up to you to see that it is all set. There is a small matter of your neck involved, also, in case anything goes wrong over the mountains!)

"Right away, sir," the yeoman answered. "The chief on the line will have it warmed up immediately. There's some sort of a rush on for this airplane, isn't there, sir?"

"Yes," I said. "Fighting Six needs it this week end for gunnery if we can get it back there."

I was already beginning to toy with the idea of flying across the country in one day. Well, why not? That flying power plant was just made for a one-day coast-to-coast. I checked out some flight gear and a parachute from the ferry locker and went outside on the apron. A long line of airplanes was warming up, being checked and inspected up and down the line while pilots stood by waiting for the mechanic's O.K. signal.

The air station at Anacostia was busy in a different way from our base at North Island. Instead of thundering formations of three, six, nine, or eighteen planes roaring in and out of the field all day long to perform their various assignments, there were only single planes maneuvering. Here is where the Navy watches the experimental planes from different factories perform before they are accepted. Here is where old planes are brought up from Norfolk after overhaul and prepared for the long flight across the country to San Diego, San Francisco, or Seattle.

This was more of a test base than anything else, and down the rows of new planes I spotted nearly every type of experimental aircraft I had read of during the past year. I could see that I was supposed to know my way around here. Everyone was busy doing his job and had little time to stop and explain or shoot the breeze with anyone else. I decided I had better go about my business of getting this airplane checked out and keep out of the way. A hot July wind swept across the runways, and most pilots were rolling up their sleeves, loosening their ties, and trying to get comfortable in the hot sun that was beating down on the concrete.

"How long do you expect to be up, sir?" the chief asked.

"About a half hour. Will you call the control tower for me?"

The chief nodded and then climbed in to start the engine.

If you have flown a fighter before it is necessary

only to adjust yourself to the new instrument board, engine operation, and various speeds of the plane. These you go over with the chief while you're turning up the engine. If everything seems in order you sign the yellow sheet and leave the chocks, but for the next half hour the smart thing to do is to try to find something wrong. It is your receipt for safe deliverance to North Island. While I was taxiing out to the runway, my eyes played on every gadget in the cockpit. As the plane picked up speed for the take-off, it wasn't hard to keep one eye on the instrument panel for any incorrect readings. They all looked O.K., and after winding up the wheels, setting the propeller pitch, stabilizer, and gas selector, I settled back against the headrest for a few minutes to enjoy what modern necessity has given to man.

At six thousand feet, after several stalls and a little feeling out of the plane to ascertain its different characteristics, I checked the radio testing with the control tower by voice and then switched to beam frequency for checks on dial settings and signal strength. Everything was "in the groove," so I took a look at the Washington Monument, the long rows of gray stone Capital buildings, the big dome itself, and started down. I had already made up my mind. If the weather was good tomorrow the sun would just be breaking out of the Atlantic as I got to altitude and headed west. I was going to race it to the Pacific—not lolling in a comfortable chair, sipping tea aboard an air liner, but plugging it myself, alone! Maybe it was some childhood dream I had had, for despite the tiresome and earsplitting hours that I knew were ahead of me, I was eager to tackle the job.

You find, on flying an airplane across the country for the first time—alone—that there are several things about flying that, despite a couple of years of flying with the Navy, you still have to learn. That is exactly why a ferry ship is such good stuff to the naval pilot. He doesn't have a section leader, division leader, squadron leader, group leader, and group commander to take charge ahead of him and do the thinking. He's got to do it himself. Weather, that uncertain shadow, is his pigeon. (I still like the term "weather" in flying as used to mean "whether," along with the visibility and ceiling conditions. To me the two terms are synonymous. It boils down to "whether" I take off to attempt the flight or "whether" I don't.) Also, the pilot on his hurried way across the United States must make his own decisions as to routes, adequate gassing facilities for his short-range fighter, best emergency fields, radio beams, beacons and frequencies, rules of the road, courses, and a host of other variables that race with him through the air—yes, even as he flies behind his complicated instruments and eyes with necessary comprehension the operation of his power plant up ahead.

I circled down over the Potomac, read the green light flashed from the tower, and rubbed the wheels along the long runway. Once more inside the operations building, I checked out maps and radio guides, the maps to be studied at the hotel during the evening. Since the weather report looked good for tomorrow all the way to Albuquerque (with even chances for that to clear), I left a call for four A.M. Sunrise would be about five ten, and by five eleven a stubby, snarling, Navy fighter should be poking its nose down the runway to wave its flippers at the rising red glow in the East.

It is still the honest desire of just about every flier in the country who hasn't had the chance to take his plane, alone, across the mountains, rivers, plains, and deserts that go to make up our broad country. If he is fortunate enough to have a fast plane and try for a coast-to-coast one-day hop, the inducement is doubled. Even in this hour of speed and express there are few planes with enough of what it takes under the engine cowl to master a fourteen-hour coast-to-coast hop. You know that. And as you sip some black coffee in the wee hours of the dewy morning some twelve hours after yesterday's check hop, you pull out the maps and make a last check to see that no time will be lost anywhere along the line.

Washington to Columbus to Kansas City. Kansas City to Wichita, Wichita to Amarillo, out over the flat Texas land to Albuquerque. Down at Winslow, Arizona, for a last tank of gas, and then out across the desert and high Lagunas to the sloping terrain that angles down to the sea at San Diego. It was a lot of air to disturb, and as my taxi jerked away from the naval air station I began to wonder. Saving three hours of daylight going west was going to help. The bad spot would be Albuquerque.

The plane was already warming up on the apron while a sleepy timekeeper checked me out.

"Weather is O.K., sir. The station clears you for

Columbus." By studying the winds aloft, the best altitude looked like ten thousand feet with a slight tail wind.

"Airways traffic gives you clearance for flight with no traffic to report on the route." (The timekeeper of a naval air base is a wonderful gent. He can get you anything but the Capitol dome when you need it!) O.K. I was set. That slight palpitation was there as I thought that if things broke right I might make a one-day flight across the country.

With a roar I was out of the field in almost a jump, and the blackness surrounding the runway behind seemed to fold itself again into solitude as I rolled up the wheels and turned the lights to low on the instrument panel. Early dawn hid the city even as the sun started to rise out of the sea. I grinned and thought, "Climb up on my back, you rascal, and I'll ride you west."

At ten thousand feet, just a few minutes later, the wings took up the red glow, throwing off an orangelike hue. The dash clock said five twenty-three, and all instruments checked O.K., with the air speed resting on 170 knots. We were moving out. Over the nose cowl through the whirling arc of the propeller were dull gray morning, the Allegheny

Mountains, and, somewhere further on, Columbus, Ohio.

With the cockpit closed it was warm, so I took off my mittens, lighted a cigarette, and watched the sun brighten up the sky and then the earth below. The air was smooth, and the engine droned a solid, muffled roar. Long green strips of mountains running north to south were broken now and then by a river or rails as I followed on the maps and noted the amount of drift caused by the wind. Lighter patches of earth showed where man had disturbed the verdant hills to claim his spot in the sun.

"Columbus—ceiling unlimited, ceiling unlimited, visibility twenty miles, visibility twenty . . ."

The Pittsburgh range was putting out the weather, and all I wanted was the ceiling and visibility at Columbus. I got it and, checking the map, found I was right on the course just along the twilight of the beam. Uniontown, Pennsylvania, nestled between the mountains backed off in the distance. Cambridge flashed by. Forty miles to go. I checked the gas supply, switched to main tank, and then stuck the nose down. The forty miles was only a scant eleven minutes, and as the wheels scraped along the concrete runway the dash clock showed seven, straight up.

Good time so far but none to waste. As the mechanics ran out the gas truck, I trotted into the office to file the arrival report and check weather at Kansas City. It was O.K., and best available wind was still at ten thousand.

"How does it look at Albuquerque?" I asked.

"No change since the early-morning report, sir. Shall I call the tower and ask them what they have?"

"No, thanks. I'll pick it up at Amarillo."

That few precious minutes' time was like water in the desert.

The tower flashed a green light as I swung around into the wind on runway two. With the throttles open the thousand horses drove out with a snarl. Seconds later I wound up the wheels, swung wide around the radio masts at the far end of the field, and put the nose on a cloud. Kansas City should be two hours ten minutes away, if no strong head winds were encountered. Ground checks over Dayton, Ohio, and St. Louis, Missouri, showed an average ground speed of over two hundred and twenty-five miles an hour.

The sun moved up higher and at ten thousand feet I was just out of the heat of a Midwestern July. The terrain below was flat, broken patches of farm land, green woods, and slicing railroad tracks that shot off into anywhere indiscriminately. It was beginning to get cramped in the cockpit, and, with the safety belt loose, I made an effort to stretch out and get the hard parachute on something else.

The minutes got longer, and I was glad to see the river make that little bend around Fairfax Airport, just across from Kansas City, where there would be at least five minutes to stretch and stand up. "Aviator's cramp" was finding another victim, and I began to realize that before this day was over the cockpit was going to grow very small.

Down the glaring white apron in front of the Naval Reserve base, I set the clock back. Two hours and twenty minutes from Columbus. Not bad. Wichita, the next stop, was only a brief fifty-five minutes away, and it was better to be off the ground up where it was cooler than standing around a hot engine in a typical Kansas sun. Whenever you drop in at a Reserve base while flying away from your own base, you make a practice of dropping in to say hello to the skipper. He usually knows a lot of the older officers, either in your squadron or others, and he's dying to hear a little about them. I was glad, though, that the captain of the base at Kansas City was out, for any time spent in talking would have cut my chances to reach North Island that night.

The mechanic pulled the chocks, and I again turned the reins over to the Cyclone. The air was still smooth, so, with the compass needle pointing correctly and the tabs set for level flight, I took my hands and feet away to find some cotton and have another smoke. The terrain below was unchanging. Minutes stretched out, seemed to hesitate. For diversion I counted with the second hand on the clock, trying to get the right interval and keep even. I checked over all the instruments, trying to find one even slightly off, but they were all pointing right. Another smoke. I switched on the radio to see how many stations it would tune in. Someone was putting out weather data back in Missouri, but it wasn't very interesting. Finally I opened the cockpit, looked out over the left wing, and picked up the outskirts of Wichita, the white crossing runways of the airport, and breathed a sigh of relief.

Down the field with a bounce, into the office with maps and reports, out again to check on the ship, and then off the ground, back up to altitude, and once more I was looking at a black instrument board with dancing needles! I spent just twenty minutes at Wichita, got the weather for Amarillo, and now was back in the harness just fifty minutes out. Clouds were piled up in the west ahead, and I kept the radio tuned in for all reports on weather in the near vicinity. The first clouds appeared to be only fat, bulky cumulus, stacked up like sky mountains, but as I got closer I could see the darkness on one side of the pack and still darker clouds in the middle. That was what might be over Albuquerque.

I tuned the radio for the Albuquerque range and got the signals faintly. A weather report came out on this range at about this time, and shortly I picked up the voice report superimposed on the beam signals.

"Albuquerque contact—ceiling two thousand feet, ceiling two thousand feet, overcast—visibility two miles, two miles—rain . . . " I switched back to the Amarillo range. Well, at least, it was contact, and I could go in if it stayed that way. But flying low around mountains with poor visibility and storm areas was nothing to gloat over. Nor did I want to take any chances with this new plane as well as my neck. The minutes dragged.

I checked the maps, keeping the radio tuned to Amarillo for checking position. By now I was almost numb on one side and long since had slipped out of the parachute, raised and lowered the seat, even tried to ignore the nagging discomfort by finding gadgets to toy with. I adjusted the mixture control again. Then the propeller pitch. On the power-control chart for the engine I figured exactly what the old bus was putting out in the way of horsepower.

Thoughts playfully entered my mind, as they always did on long formation flights with the squadron. "Suppose the right wing suddenly tore away. I'll bet I could get over the side where the wing isn't. No. It would be better to try the other side. We'd spin that way, and I'd get a prop in my neck."

With the cockpit cover tightly closed I tried to sing like Crosby. The low notes wouldn't come out, because the engine roar drowned them, so I just screamed in silence! Another smoke. I shifted the seat again and now was almost lying down—feet out beyond the rudder bars and knees rubbing the stick. The increase in comfort was about nil, and a few minutes later I was sitting up straight, watching the approaching rain clouds shadow the earth far up ahead. The instrument pointers jiggled in their cases, and I wished they would settle down for a while.

The terrain below was now a continuous unbroken stretch of reddish field clay and sand-colored rocks. Now and then a spot of green surrounded a thin, trickling stream, and a few nobs of low mountains prodded out here and there. Again I argued that it would be sensible to sit down at Albuquerque for a rest—spend the night and then push on to North Island the next day before noon. (It is nice to think about stopping, but you know you will keep on.) I began to wonder if any of the boys back at the air base had their transfer orders yet. Had Noz got Pearl Harbor, as he had wanted?

The field at Amarillo was without runways and very muddy from recent rains. The wheels threw the chocolate high in the air, splattering the wings as I half taxied, half slid up to the small concrete driveway used for an apron. As the mechanics started to gas the mud- and oil-streaked fighter, I pushed past a small gathering of gaping laymen, into the two-by-four shanty to file the arrival and departure reports. The usual salutations and friendly wisecracks were omitted as I wiped the oil from my goggles and got the dope on the weather.

"Yep. The field at Albuquerque is O.K. now. It has been raining there all morning, but the stuff has moved east and south. We ought to be getting some sprinkles here before long." The red-faced, khaki-clothed radioman was glad for the chance to talk a little shop. He explained that most of the planes went right past Amarillo to Albuquerque, and only the small jobs dropped in.

"Man, you've been carrying the mail, haven't you?" He caught a glimpse of the smoking breather pipes and the exhaust-blackened fuselage. I said I hadn't wasted any time and was trying for the coast by sundown. He rubbed his stubble. "That's some order, but then that's some airplane, too," he said and went out to get a look at the cockpit.

Minutes were still precious, and it was already one thirty-five. Just around the corner from the weather shack I found a small cafe converted from a house, and the sandwiches tasted better than I believed possible. A gulp of coffee, a piece of candy for the next few long hours, and within twenty minutes I was back in the cockpit, ears still ringing, to struggle with the shotgun starter and a change of maps for the last three legs.

With a growl I was out of the hot, sticky field, pointing the nose west, and catching more sun in the cockpit as the race drew closer against the speeding, eternal clock in the sky. But the coffee and sandwiches had helped, and now I affected a grim determination to make the coast by six thirty or bust. The day seemed old, the time long since I had climbed out of the field at Anacostia to watch the day break across the Alleghenies, and I began to realize how much there was to flying a ferry hop coast to coast in one day. With the parachute slipped forward and almost under my knees, the relief was gratifying, and with hunched shoulders I awaited the first streaks of water on the windshield as the clouds started to get under the wing and around to the south.

There it came! Drops splattered against the glass house to shiver off across the edges. I nosed over. Time to drop down through the clouds and mist to stay in contact with the ground. The air got rough fast, and with the safety belt pulled tight I still bounced against the sides of the cockpit and glass house. The soothing feeling of aloneness in a storm with a dry roof overhead produced thought food for the moment, but that was rudely interrupted. The carburetor air temperature dropped to fifteen degrees. Ice! With the heat full on, it slowly climbed back to thirty-two, but I kept rechecking to make sure we wouldn't get any more. That's the stuff forced landings are made of!

Roar, roar, roar. The mountains, jutting up almost to the overcast, were wet and the rocks slick with trickling water. At twenty-five hundred feet I had to keep alert to check the terrain, for a two hundred-mile speed gives you just so much time to trace a river or railroad at low altitude. By switching to the Albuquerque beam I double-checked against the maps for a short time, but hanging on the right-hand side of the beam and staring through the streaming windshield took all my time, so I stuffed the maps back into the case and hung on the beam. The compass needle danced in the rough air. I was very tired but almost too busy to notice it.

Minutes later the three fields at Albuquerque showed up in the flat ahead just on the edge of the storm area, and sunshine was almost on the town itself, sparkling down past the black clouds to the wet earth. I picked out the large unfinished air terminal to the southeast of town, wishing that it were completed. Across the river to the west, an air liner was going into the field I wanted, and I swung wide behind him until he had taxied up to the loading platform in front of the airport. Then I dropped down to the wet sand runways and splashed up to the gas truck. The sky was broken and blue in spots, and the sun struck down like golden arrows at the flat sand and squatty dunes. What a relief to see clear sky ahead and think about getting back to the base.

Inside the office building the teletype punched and rattled out its broken lines of symbols and words. Winslow, Arizona, Burbank unlimited, San Diego high overcast, ceiling five thousand, visibility fifteen miles. That's plenty. Nothing could stop me now, nothing but trouble with the plane, and so far that engine with a seat had performed like a master. There were five hours of daylight remaining, so it looked like a party at the mess tonight and a blowout for the boys. My back was sore and the ears rung like doorbells, but again I thought what a sissy I was if I couldn't take fourteen hours, when Lindbergh, Post, and Corrigan could still grin after some twenty-five or thirty.

The runway was dotted with puddles of brown water, and the wheels tossed the spray over the wings and cockpit as I whipped down the strip ahead of the departing air liner. San Diego before sundown. Regulations say, "You will land an hour before sundown," so with the throttle pushed open to maximum I started up for altitude, hoping the wind data they gave me were correct.

The sun had moved out on the nose now, and the glare forced the proverbial "squint-eye." With the cockpit open and with my goggles on it was a bit better, so I pulled on my mittens, tucked the scarf around closer, and closed the air regulator. The engine roar actually seemed like silence. So I wanted to fly the country in one day! Well, here it was, and as I looked at the winding road below with its crawling omnibuses the thought of the wagon-trail days, with their six months' crossing, popped into the picture.

I rested my chin on the side of the cowl and, gazing down at the snaking highway, tried to visualize the old wagon train, oxen and all, plodding along over all that land I had crossed today. With a look at the instruments and their flickering needles again, the future replaced the past. How far will we go in flying? War was already spurting airplane performance and speeds to dizzy numbers, even in *"fast"* talk. What would we see forty years from now?

Winslow, Arizona. Out of the flat country into the rough. It seemed as if I had flown for twenty days with no rest, and my mind was almost a dull blank. Interest in anything but getting home had gone with the hours. Even the thought of being one of the boys on the base who had flown the country in one day had lost its appeal. Down on the sand for gas and oil. Into the office for reports, weather. The lanky radio operator, weather man, and general all-round superintendent of his lonesome retreat was not fully awake as I signed a departure report and started out.

He lowered his long legs from the desk and

drawled, "Want this sent to North Island, don't you?" I told him I did and also to Albuquerque, for information. He shoved the latest weather sequence across his marked-up desk, and I checked it over. Then I was off again and up into the ether.

The sun was down low, starting to turn deep red. Out across the Imperial Desert with its furrowed sand. Over Salton Sea, which sinks several hundred feet below sea level, and across the spa of Palm Springs, beneath the very shadow of the nine thousand-foot mountains, the Lagunas. Home was just beyond that range! I could see the boys back at the base now, walking down along the edge of the field to the officers' mess hall. Beany was probably getting set to run in town to a movie right after supper, and Bunky, Noz, Kane, and some of the more social of the gang were more than likely on the phone trying to get dates for the station movie.

Incidentally, the station movie is a very fine theater of entertainment on any air base. Here you can see all the best movies of the year, if you don't mind taking them a couple of months late. What's more, it costs you the princely sum of one penny to attend! We used to accuse the boys who took dates to the station movie of being close to tying the knot and of saving their money for the "home that was planned" or "those future 'little' things." Two cents wasn't much to spend on a date! It is in this same station theater that plays are put on for benefits by Navy wives, lectures are heard, and also last rites are held for the shipmate who just "went in." We did spend some very joyful nights at the officers' station movie, clapping for the villain and hissing the hero.

Some of the squadrons were probably taking off for night flying about this time, to spread the growling and roaring of several scores of airplanes out across the town of Coronado, even across the bay to San Diego. One by one, around ten o'clock, their twinkling red and green running lights would round the edge of the golf course on the Coronado side of Spanish Bight to swing in over the patrol hangars and settle down on the field. Then it would be quiet again for the townfolk.

The stubby nose of the fighter pushed over the highest ridge along the edge of the desert.

My back was very tired now and threatened to stay in the stooped position, and my right leg slept peacefully. It didn't seem as if minutes could be so long, and I gave up trying to amuse myself. Just hang on and wait. The air was still rough, jolting and growing colder as the sun sank lower and lower. Below, the mountains turned deep gray and purple around their bases as the lengthening shadows sneaked across the valley to inject duskiness. But the country from here in was familiar, and I watched the big silver dome of the Palomar Observatory pass under—then strained for a white strip in the approaching dusk that would be the surf of the Pacific meeting the coast.

With left hand on the stick and pad and pencil on the right knee, I added up actual flying time from Anacostia. Thirteen hours thirty-four minutes! The clock, set back to Pacific Coast time, showed six ten, and the sun out in the ocean had just begun to dip below the horizon. La Jolla, Point Loma, and finally the lights of San Diego showed up under the wing, and just across the bay the big searchlight on the tower at North Island made its rounds. Down went the wheels for the last time. Instruments checked O.K., gas on reserve, propeller in low pitch. Several destroyers were filing into the bay through the channel around the point. Their day's maneuver was over, too, and their crews would be glad for the rest and peace of the evening.

"North Island tower to Navy fourteen sixty-seven—the mat is clear to land southwest."

The sun was down low in the ocean, and I knew I was on the short side of that "hour before dark" regulation but not enough to worry about. I slipped into the field across Spanish Bight to land short on the black asphalt mat in front of Operations. It was a welcome sight to see the mechanic motion my oil- and mud-spattered fighter up easily against the chocks as I jotted down the last figure on the knee pad.

"Landed at North Island six twenty-two. Turned plane into aircraft battle-force pool for distribution to fleet forces."

I don't know when I was quite so whipped down and deaf from continuously flying hour after hour with hardly a break—even during our long formation flights. True, it was great stuff to sit down that night with Bud and the boys and think that I had actually navigated the whole country in one day on my first ferry trip, and I had learned a lot. Figuring speeds, time of arrivals, playing smart with the weather forecasts, and going into different fields along the way all gave just a bit more of a "finish" to my aviation. It was another step along the road of flying at an air base that was meant to be a definite part of my training.

But before I had more than sunk into the soft leather of an armchair I was nodding like grampa in his rocker. And I was sore for three days. The next time a ferry trip showed up I made up my mind to take things just a little easier. McClure and Mead and several of the older pilots of the squadron smiled when I told them about flying the "whole works" in one day. They knew what that kind of "pushing" does to a pilot. I hadn't known. But when I thought back about how numb and unobservant a person can get after flying too long at one stretch I realized that I had learned another lesson.

By the end of August Bombing Two had completed two weeks of fixed gunnery, fired for record, and begun the current dive-bombing practice for the year. We didn't do so badly either. There were seven freshly painted "E's" (for efficiency) over the names of three old pilots and four young recruits when the smoke from the machine-gun fire had been wiped from the fuselages. The four young recruits were "proud like anything," and since the same reports were coming in from other squadrons' firing-record practices, we all felt just a little chesty about keeping the older boys hopping. But high score still went to Lieutenant McClure, and I was glad.

Mac had been the hardest working, most conscientious person in fleet aviation I had ever met, and he deserved all those holes he put in the target. His red-nosed bullets had ripped eighty-seven gashes in the white canvas sleeve out of a possible one hundred and twelve. Take it from me, that is some shooting. When you point an airplane at a target sleeve far below, roll around it, and come up under with eyes glued to the sight, waiting to push your fire button on top of the stick, it is going to take all the smooth flying and skill your brain can relay to your arms and legs.

All this is not done from one approach, where you could eventually get things lined up and be sure of hits. It isn't quite so simple. There are five or six various "attacks" to be made on the target that require various maneuvers from loops and Immelmans to push-over dives before that elusive little "sock" the tow plane is pulling will come into your ring sight. And then you have to allow the right lead, or you will come back to the base and swear a pink streak that "at least two strings of those tracers went right through the target. I know they did. I saw 'em!" The tow plane drops the target, and when you rush over to pick it up, to your utter chagrin "there isn't a hole in the damned thing!"

I finally got the news, though, and when we completed our record bombing a couple of weeks later I was strutting along with Alex, McClure, Stephens, and Ewers to have the painter do an "extra-special job" when he painted the "E" on the fuselage. And these "E" marks, which stand for efficiency, are some of the things that a pilot on an air base will fight for. They mean something to him, and the spirit of the practice, real efficiency at gunnery, bombing, radio communications, and such, are the type of thing a red-blooded pilot lives by.

I've seen many lieutenant commanders and even commanders argue to high heaven, "It's a green spot, I tell you, you can see where it starts in the target that it's left a green stain, and I was shooting green-painted bullets!" Or, "Now, Frank, you can see as well as I that that first mark in the target is yellow, and this is burned powder, not green paint, you are looking at."

If the hit they are arguing about is a draw, then someone flips a coin, and all is forgotten. Their hearts and souls are in this business, and they are doing the best that is in them to be good so that when the time comes to fire at a real enemy plane or bomb a real enemy base they will be there with the goods—and be able to deliver. Most of the boys know that, too. They take their practices around the base seriously, month after month, and if you think your team back at old Goal-line College worked to be champions, you should watch the pilots at an air base practice to become champions at their game!

And sometimes they work too hard, get a bit overenthusiastic, and "hold on" that fatal last second in a dive. Then you have the things that happened to Smitty happening all over again. Stephens, as fine an officer and pilot as ever became a naval aviator, needed one more "close one" for an "E," not three weeks after I left the fleet. He grimly held on in a vertical dive, keeping the nose of his plane pointed right at the bull's-eye a fraction of a second too long. His pull-out was one-half completed when he hit the hard sand at the edge of the bombing target at Border Field, burying the engine six feet in the ground. It was his last close one.

You may wonder about this flirting with death for a hit flying, and why one would take such a chance. When you squint through the sight, watching the target grow bigger and bigger, there is a terrific urge to hang on just a bit longer before jerking the bomb release and getting out of your dive. You feel certain that "just a fraction longer" and your aim will be perfect, and the screaming whine of the plane as the speed leaps up is secondary to your concentration on that fast-growing bull's-eye.

I suppose you should remember while flying around an air base, practicing gunnery and bombing, that old adage, "He who fights and runs away may live to fight another day!" There were seven boys I knew who I wish had thought of it. Peace be with them for remembering too well, "Better to have tried and lost than never to have tried at all!"

Chapter XIII

During the last few years the operations carried on aboard the air station at North Island have been fraught with increasing experimental practice along with the usual short cruises, bombing, gunnery, and aerial combat work. As the tempo of the preparedness program speeded up, so did the flying on the base, both day and night.

One day you might read a dispatch from commander air battle force that would say to expedite firing long-range machine-gun fire at a towed target in conjunction with another squadron. And then you might spend two weeks squinting through your telescope sight at a "sock" that appeared no bigger than a pea. You would line it up as deftly and accurately as possible, squeeze the trigger button, and spurt a stream of tracers through a couple of thousand feet of free air. They would dart into, under, and over the target, and you could watch them raise tiny geysers out of the sea below as they spent themselves. Then, with the answers on range, possible hits, and the practicability of such long-distance firing written up and sent to commander air battle force, the squadron would be assigned some other "trial" practice.

One week we flew every night, doing dive bombing by section formation of three planes, finding out the possibilities of night formation dive bombing. To me that is still about the most hazardous flying I ever did while attached to the air base at North Island. Out we would go, three planes at a time, in V formation, with the radio humming and crackling through the earphones from the moment we left the line until all planes had landed again. And it was necessary chatter that went out over the air on those nights.

Night flying in formation is far from easy any time, and when you read about the dogfights that go on over England in the inky blackness you can bet the air is also full of tension. Judging distance in the air at night is the hardest job of all. The yellow formation lights and the green and red running lights of the section leader look far off as you close in on him to join up. Then suddenly they are right there below and in front of the nose, and you jerk off the throttle, strain through the engulfing blackness, and try to hold your plane back from shooting right on past him. Collisions can occur at any time that the pilot of any plane in the vicinity of another relaxes his strict vigilance for one fleeting second. If you were to go out on one of these night flights with a section, here is what you would probably find as the mechanic gave you a thumbs-up, pulled the chocks, and waved you down the taxi strip after the flaming exhausts of the plane ahead.

"North Island tower to Bombing Two—the field is clear for take-off" comes through the earphones. The rendezvous has already been decided, so you sit waiting in the surrounding blackness as Number One pours on the coal, spits yellow and blue flames from open exhausts, and roars off into the night. You can follow his running lights as they bounce over the mat, then smooth out, and slant against the blackness as the pilot banks his plane in a climbing turn. Then Number Two follows, and you swing the nose around to point down the mat at nothing and push home the throttle.

The point is to keep an eye on those red and green lights circling up ahead and join up slowly and easily when the rendezvous point is reached. It makes it easier, for there is no accurate way of telling at night whom you are joining up with. And your face can get very red if you fly along after a pair of twinkling running lights to pull up after a hard chase and see some strange-colored tail section glare up at you instead of your own. It happens now and then.

So after you pull up the wheels, set the propeller pitch, change the fuel-tank selector, and check over the instruments, you will want to turn the lights on the instrument panel down low to get away from the glare and keep your eyes peeled for other planes as well as those two you are following.

Below, if you are out over the ocean, is a black void that shows nothing, unless the moon is bright. But back toward the shore the lights from the cities of San Diego and Coronado will make it doubly hard to follow those of the first two planes. All this time, when other squadrons are operating on night-tactics missions, the air will be alive with calls.

"Fighting Two, join up over lower bay at six thousand in left-hand circles," comes a terse command.

"Scouting Two to North Island—we are breaking up north of Point Loma over Mission Bay and will come into the landing circle in about four minutes."

The base answers back with instructions or a receipt, and someone else opens up from another squadron. If night carrier landings are being made on the field the signal officer gets in a few messages now and then. All transmission is brief and to the point. If a crash occurs on the field during a landing, the word is passed first by radio, then supplemented with red flares that are sent up from a "crash truck," to warn all other planes to stand clear until further instructions are received.

Every night flight I made after that first evening aboard the station—when Bud and I watched in awe as two dripping flyers pulled themselves out of their rubber boat—on every flight I have wondered about night forced landings. Many times I would sit there staring at the eerie fuselage of the plane ahead, automatically moving the controls in the roaring blackness, while my mind toyed with the questions, "What to do, pilot, if your engine quits? What to do, quick and decisively? What to do first?" I wonder now if those questions were ever answered, for such answers change with every flight, every hour, every minute in aviation. You have to be even more on your toes every minute of night flying, and the strain is wearing after only one hour.

Your section leader leads you out over the target, which shows several white lights for identification, and your eyes never leave the glimmering fuselage of his plane. All maneuvers are gradual and easy. Even those can fool you at times.

One of the boys in a fighting squadron was doing formation maneuvers behind his section leader one night out over Point Loma, when he had an uneasy feeling. Was his section leader flying in a tight turn? He was certain something was wrong. When the lights of San Diego glared out beyond the leading plane, cocked up at an angle, he was positive that they were flying in a steep turn, nearly on their backs! That was enough for him, and his senses just wouldn't take any more. He pulled his plane up and away from the formation, trying in his mind to get everything right side up! Suddenly he fell against the belt, hung there, and then got cold in his stomach. He was upside down! That night at the mess hall he told us what had gone on.

"I knew there wasn't much altitude to waste, because we had been flying at four thousand feet," he said. "That really had me worried, because just as I got things straight and knew my plane was inverted the motor quit cold. All I could do was pull the nose down and hope there was enough sky to get around in. When I got to the bottom of the half loop and straightened out the altimeter read six hundred feet, and I was a little weak all over. Boy, that water is black! And what a hell of a feeling to be diving down at it, hoping you could get around and in level flight before it came up and hit you!"

This same chap, a few months later, finished his tour of duty with me and went to Sweden to test fighter planes for the Swedish air corps. I saw him one night shortly after his return, and we sat around his hotel room talking over old times. He still remembers his close one that night back at North Island.

When your hour of night flying is nearly over the

section leader checks his watch time with the tower to be sure there is no error in landing time. Then he leads you back close to the field and calls the tower for the last time.

"Two Baker Six to North Island, last section Bombing Two breaking up to land. We will be in the traffic lane in about three minutes."

Then you slide cautiously over into echelon, lower your wheels and flaps—and, with a blink of his lights, Number One falls away and heads for the field. Leaving just enough interval so as not to crowd into his slip stream, you follow, dropping down and watching for the floodlights to come on. They light the black asphalt to a grayish glow, and you can just make out the flitting silhouette of Number One crossing the bight at the edge of the field. Then you swing low over the edge of the field, switch on the landing light, and bounce the wheels down with a squeal. After the last plane has landed, off go the floodlights, and your part of the night-flying schedule is completed.

Peculiarly enough, few accidents occur during these operations, mostly, I believe, because everyone is paying strictest attention to business. Every pilot knows how easily and quickly a collision can occur at night, when you can't see anything but sputtering exhausts, dimly mirrored fuselages, and now and then the thousand confusing lights of the city. So Uncle Sam loses relatively few aircraft or pilots from accidents occurring while night flying is in progress.

It is interesting to look back on a few years of life spent aboard an air base. There were so many of these interesting things that went on day by day, so many little incidents to make up the human side of your existence that now, to me, those three years seem like three months. It isn't just a big game, full of flag waving and drama, and the bands don't play or the crowds cheer when you do a good job at some particular task. A short note of commendation from the commandant, a word from your captain, or a "nice going" from your shipmates, and that is all. You go on flying, doing your part with your squadron, both in the air and on the ground, and the reward that comes is the feeling of satisfaction that "it was a job well done." So if you miss a pat on the back and feel a bit mistreated at first, you soon learn that the respect you quietly received for that job "well done" speaks louder than words.

Flight operations on an air base go on at a humming pace right up to Saturday noon, and then all the Navy, for the most part, stops all flying until Monday. If you aren't standing a "watch" or haven't caught the squadron duty, your time is your own to relax and play. The Navy knows the importance of physical fitness among its officers and men, and it stops at nothing to put every recreational facility at your disposal. About once a month our whole squadron of some hundred and fifty men would set out for the beach and spend a whole day on a picnic to forget airplanes, duties, regulations, and rank. It served to take the edge off a fast-moving, hard-flying group of individuals who knew, with the ever-increasing war rumbling, the meaning of the word "efficiency."

One week we were preparing to go aboard the carrier for a few days of practice cruise with other units of the fleet—out into the Pacific to give battle to the "enemy," reported by the long-range patrol planes; the next week, back at the base in time to start a week of gunnery or bombing practice. Several times every year there is radio-code competition, in which you gather around the long green squadron table to make as few mistakes as possible, jotting down the letters for those dots and dashes the man sends out from the head of the table. That is simply to determine the most proficient squadron at radio sending and receiving at the base, but all year long you have been practicing sending out messages to one another once a day. This is done at odd hours between flights, when there is a little spare time.

All in all, your squadrons on an air base form into a compact, self-retaining group of individuals, whose interests are the same—both at work and at play. In flight there are eighteen men all working as a team, concentrating on the job ahead and anticipating from flying associations what the other seventeen will do. After the day's or week's operations are over, that same squadron interest can be a dinner, a picnic, a dance, or just plain get-together at someone's house. When a new member arrives, replacing someone in the organization, he soon finds he is among friends and is shortly at home with his new shipmates. Not that you don't see a lot of the boys from the other squadrons on the field—you do. But the functions of your own unit take up most of your time.

On week ends at North Island, for a change of scenery, you might go anywhere.

"I wonder is there is anything to this Death Valley Scotty story you hear so much about," Bud said one Saturday afternoon.

"I don't know," Vensel said, "but why don't we go up there and find out?"

Bud came out with his usual, "Well, what are we waiting for?" And off we went to pile, one and all, into faithful "Hotdamn" and make a fast trip to the desert to call on Mr. Scotty.

Many times we used to hop down across the border into Tijuana, some fifteen miles away, and listen to the songs of Old Mexico, done up the native way. We had to stop that when some of the Mexicans decided to stage a few riots around the Tijuana jail and began to shoot up everything they laid eyes on. I was really worried about little Beany, who I was afraid might decide to take on the whole gang of rioters at once!

I suppose a riot in the air is one of the unusual calamities that might occur on an air base or flying field. But we had the next thing to it in the sky around North Island one afternoon while a Marine squadron was out practicing gunnery runs on a towed target sleeve. The story, now almost a legend, is one of the best the air base has to offer, and it all happened like this:

Three Marine planes were making practice dives on a white target sleeve being towed by a fourth plane in the group. They were doing their runs in an area over land, because they weren't firing any guns and were just getting some familiarization dives. The three planes would simply dive down from above at the white sleeve, sight through their telescope sights, and then try to get in close to the target before pulling out, simulating actual firing conditions. One of the planes misjudged and came too close to the white canvas sleeve, and the next thing he knew there was a tug on his wing, and about twenty feet of cable and canvas was wrapped around the wing tip.

Sometimes diving into a target sleeve isn't serious, but this time it was. The pilot had no control of his airplane because the target sleeve was wound around one of the control surfaces on the end of the wing. He immediately tried to shake it free but couldn't and, noticing that there were only about five thousand feet between him and the ground, yelled back to his mechanic to bail out. He continued to fight the plane along on a steady course. The mechanic loosened his safety belt and climbed over the side, pulling his rip cord at the same time and floating away from the plane. When he was clear the pilot prepared to do the same and loosened his belt, stood up in the seat, and got one leg over the cockpit. Then, just as he was about to jump, he felt the plane give a slight jerk and noticed that the target that had fouled his controls had torn loose and was floating away from the plane. So back he climbed into the cockpit, fastened his safety belt, and headed the plane for North Island.

All the time this was going on, the leader of the three-plane section had been watching from several thousand feet above, unable to do anything more than hope that both occupants of the crippled plane got free. He saw from his position one white parachute blossom forth from the falling plane, so he picked up his microphone and called the base.

"North Island from Marine Plane One—Marine Plane Three just hit the target sleeve over Camp Kearney. One of the crew has bailed out, and his chute opened O.K. The plane is still circling down, and I am waiting for the pilot to bail out."

The section leader couldn't see too clearly from his position, several thousand feet above the falling plane. He watched the crippled plane as the mechanic's chute opened and floated away. "Come on, leatherneck! Get out of there yourself," he muttered, waiting for the white, mushrooming silk of his brother officer to show up. "There! That's the boy," he thought to himself as a second "white" dot blew away from the crippled plane and floated toward the mesa below. The target sleeve had torn free.

Several seconds later he called again on the radio, "North Island from Marine Plane One—the second occupant has just bailed out, and his chute opened O.K., too. The plane is now diving in the general direction of North Island, and I will try to follow it until it crashes." Then he thought, "Better warn everybody," and opened up on the radio again.

"All planes in the air from Marine One. A pilotless plane is in the air between Camp Kearney and North Island, heading in the direction of the Silver Strand. All planes be on the lookout for a pilotless plane! Both occupants have bailed out."

The piece of target tearing away from the wing had looked like a parachute to him!

In the meantime, the pilot of the "nearly abandoned" aircraft was on his merry way for North Island. He had no idea what was going on over the radio, because his hands were full getting his plane down safely and quickly to report the accident and the whereabouts of his mechanic, who by this time had landed safely just south of the field. When he flew over the Silver Strand to get into the landing groove, planes began to scatter. Everyone was trying to get out of the way of the "pilotless" airplane of Marine Squadron Two! The radio was alive with frantic calls.

"Pilotless plane is coming down the groove below the hotel! Pilotless plane in the groove along the Silver Strand! Marine plane without pilot heading for North Island is almost to South Field. All planes beware!"

The havoc created by the ghost ship without a pilot was terrific. Planes, section formations, single planes, flying boats, seaplanes, all swung wide and scattered, as poor, unmindful Marine Plane Three came around the breakwater, crossed over Spanish Bight, and landed on the field at West Beach. The poor pilot, who had lost the ear cord from his radio when he stood up to bail out, was completely oblivious of all the commotion he was causing.

The only thing he couldn't figure out, he told us later, was why everyone dived out of his way and cleared the sky! Usually you had to pick and worry your way through the traffic back to the field! After he reached the line and cut the engine, he found out what was going on, for immediately his squadron mates rushed out to get the news. Then he didn't know whether to laugh about the whole thing or take it seriously!

When the news got around the air base, the laughs were on. We had a big time teasing the pilot who reported, "Both occupants have bailed out, and the plane is diving toward North Island!" We promptly nicknamed the big, blond marine who flew the heralded ship back "Ghost!" The story of that escapade is a legend now around the fleet, and you can hear it from any flyer who has been around North Island for any length of time. It was one of those amusing incidents that helped to even the score of the serious mishaps that are inevitable when a group of hundreds of planes fly on various missions from one base.

Some three or four months before we left the fleet most of us were wondering about what we were going to do and where we were going to do it. Our active duty was about over, and Uncle Sam had some forty more Reserves, all with nearly fifteen hundred hours of flying time and a lot of good experience behind us. We were looking for jobs. We had no idea how eager some of the air lines were to seize on this opportunity to fill their expanding rosters, but shortly before we ended our duty with the fleet they began sending out applications.

What were they getting? Just this. A pilot of irreproachable skill, with from fifteen hundred to two thousand hours of the toughest yet most delicate flying there is; a graduate of one of the world's best flight-training schools; an officer who knew how to take orders and how to give them; a navigator and radioman, as well as a pilot; and more— a man who had learned the value of that term that air lines capitalize at all times—"teamwork." (Nearly half of the first two classes to leave the fleet went to a large air line back in the Middle West, which boasted of being an organization built by pilots. It was, and the members of my class who are flying for that company are more than satisfied, for flying is their business.)

Some of the boys found different opportunities awaiting them, but to this day I don't know of a one who isn't involved in some angle of flying. As it turned out, Bud, my big leatherneck friend, started out for an air-line job that looked good to him, and I jumped at a chance to go to France as a test pilot. This was for the French Navy, in conjunction with an American aircraft plant, selling dive bombers to the French.

I spent six months hustling back and forth between Paris and Brest to find all the parts for all the airplanes.

They were scattered to kingdom come, arriving at any port, because of the necessity of dodging German submarines and raiders on the way over. We ended up getting all the planes flown, but minus an odd part here and there. At that, the Frenchmen were almost in tears at receiving such *"joli"* aircraft to replace what they had. And they had something worse than nothing. One of the squadrons at Brest, which was to be based aboard the old carrier *Béarn*, was still flying antiquated Levasseur P.L. 7's, which staggered into the air behind an old

Hispano-Suiza motor. The commanding officer asked me one day if I would like to fly one, adding with a smile, "To see why it is we are in great need of your new ships."

I crawled into the cockpit of this three-place torpedo bomber, tested the sputtering engine, took two looks at the rusted control cables, the "bailing-wire" wrapping on the *longérons*—and shut off the engine. Maybe I'm a sissy, but there wasn't one safe-looking reason why I should fly that airplane! I could see what "*le capitaine*" meant without even taxiing it away from the hangar!

However, the French air base at Brest was laid out along the lines of our own air station at Norfolk, and unlike the flying equipment found there, the base itself was modern, the hangars, officers' quarters, and seaplane docks well planned and up-to-date. If they had had a few thousand of our newest airplanes at this base and at all the other bases in France, the story of Belgium and Holland might have been different. There is not a word of adverse comment that anyone can make about the skill and daring of the French pilots. Those that there were when the war got away to its belated start put everything they had into an attempt to stop the German tanks. They went out in all the Curtisses, Voughts, and Douglases they could find to fly. The rest took whatever was left that had wings —and the carnage was terrific! Of the nine officers and men I know in one squadron of fourteen, not one came out of the "push to Paris" alive! The two mechanics and I came home after six months, happy that our job was completed and not too eager to see what we knew must be inevitable. I reported back to the aircraft factory and went on test flying.

When we left North Island we all ended up with flying jobs that more or less suited our tastes. And why shouldn't we? Uncle Sam had spent some twenty-five thousand dollars training each of us to be the best flyers in the world. We had been aboard an active, fast-operating air base, doing actual fleet and combat maneuvers, and our training was by this time pretty thorough. We were proud of it, too, and today as the country stands at the brink of a possible two-ocean war, all those officers trained from North Island and several other large bases around the country are simply standing by to be called back to active duty. They are ready to fulfill the jobs for which Uncle Sam trained them, and simply stepped out at the end of four years to allow room for the new ones coming up.

That is the way the United States has built a naval air force of no mean proportions in the past six years, and you will find at nearly every air line, aircraft company, and airplane factory pilots from some air base or air station, trained and ready to resume their former roles as fighting pilots if and when they are called. Each month the Naval Reserve pilot on inactive duty (not actually attached to a fleet unit or actively operating squadron) reports to his Naval Reserve aviation base, where he keeps his hand in at flying and maneuvering the fast combat planes Uncle Sam is getting. When the time comes for him to report to his squadron and go out to meet the aggressor, this Reserve pilot will be no novice at the game.

And now, as I conclude, war seems even more imminent for the United States. President Roosevelt has declared a "state of unlimited emergency" for the whole country. Everywhere you look factories are expanding to the limit to turn out untold supplies of war materials and, above all, planes, planes, and more planes. Flying fields everywhere are being conditioned, to be used for training, or

AIR BASE

are being turned over to the Army or the Navy for actual defense purposes of our country. After what happened at Crete, there is little doubt in anyone's mind just how important air control in time of war or adequate air bases for swift operation really are.

Not long ago the huge flying field, Floyd Bennett, at Brooklyn, New York, was commissioned as a United States naval air station. That happened on June 2, 1941, and three of us Naval Reserve officers were honored when the commanding officer asked us to participate in the commissioning ceremonies. Before attempting our small part of the flying events we sat out in front of the huge administration building, facing the concrete apron, on which were spaced row upon row of the fastest and newest naval fighting aircraft the country had. I listened attentively while the fiery little mayor of New York, Fiorello H. LaGuardia, turned the long-time commercial field over to the Navy's Rear Admiral Adolphus Andrews, commandant of the district.

"I am happy to turn over to the United States Navy one of New York's most cherished possessions," said the mayor. "It is to be used as a base of operations of neutrality patrol and, even more, as a base of protection for the coast of the United States." I could just make out, on the clear and balmy day, the distant outline of Manhattan's sky wall of spires and towers. "Most of you," he went on to the overflowing crowd of eager spectators, "have homes which are but a scant four or five minutes away from this field by air. To you, as well as to the surrounding coast line and territorial waters, this base will prove another step toward defending those homes and families you so rightfully love."

When the commanding officer-to-be of the new air station, Commander Don Smith, finished reading his orders from Washington, which made him captain of the base, the aerial demonstration began. Nine P-40 Curtiss Pursuit ships blazed down across the long field in front of the lines of people who surged close to the restricting fences. The Army Air Corps, summoned from Mitchel Field on Long Island, were right on time. As Commander Smith finished reading his orders, he turned and briskly snapped to attention with a smart salute. "Admiral Towers, I hereby assume duty as captain of the United States naval air station, Floyd Bennett Field, Brooklyn, New York."

The P-40's had timed it just right. The nine of them streaked down out of nowhere to level off some thirty feet above the ground in a formation of V's and roar across the field. They pulled up steeply, swung around in perfect formation, and came back over the field to do some Lufberry circles and tail-chasing antics. Following them came three huge Consolidated Flying Boats, which were housed in the big hangars at the far side of the field. They were painted sea blue like the ocean, a camouflage that is effectively used by patrol planes on the neutrality patrols, and are hard to spot from above while flying over the water. The pilots held a nice, close formation as they brought their stately craft down low across the runways to rumble off toward the sea.

The crowd didn't know it, but these flying boats were actually on their way then to take up their stations far out over the ocean and begin another patrol. We donned our flight gear and walked out to our planes, which were already warming up in the center of the mile-long parking apron. I was thinking about Floyd Bennett, the unselfish hero for whom this field had been named, the former Navy man who had sacrificed his life in an attempt to fly a rescue plane through the cold north to aid his fellow men. I wondered what he would think if he could see the majestic sight of "his" air field being given to Uncle Sam—once again to "aid his fellow men."

Then, after the three of us took off to do a few section formation maneuvers and dive down low, past the surging crowd along the apron and hangars in a roaring salute, I thought back to those days at North Island. I wondered if that huge crowd down there knew of the real "blood and sweat" that would go into making this newly commissioned airport an efficient air base. I wondered if they knew of the little incidents, the tragedies, the heroics, and the everyday operations that would go on here now to make another "North Island" for the country's defense.

It is for those who may not know what goes on aboard an "air base"—that small world in itself—that this book is written. For in my opinion it is on those vital centers of air coordination, those stations that harbor our air fleets that the actual fate of this country in a war with aggressor nations will depend.

I am leaving myself wide open, when I say—and I firmly believe—that air power will shortly assume such strength that land and sea operations can hope only to be the "mopping up" after the bombers have completed their mission and the fighters take control of the sky. The huge new air bases that are springing up in the territories around our country are the most vital concern of our whole defense program. The men who fly from them are, to my mind, the actual bulwark of a defense against any *Luftwaffe* to approach these shores. I am wondering now at the astounding foresight of Thomas Gray, who wrote the following verse just two hundred years ago. It was translated from his *Luna Habitalis*, written in Latin. I wonder, for it strikes close to home.

> The time will come, when thou shalt lift thine eyes
> To watch a long-drawn battle in the skies,
> While aged peasants, too amazed for words,
> Stare at the flying fleets of wond'rous birds.
> England, so long the mistress of the sea,
> Where winds and waves confess her sovereignty,
> Her ancient triumphs yet on high shall bear,
> And reign, the sovereign of the conquered air.

Index

A

Air bases, adequate, importance of, 279
  center of air coordination, 282
  East Coast, 223
  function of, 93
  life aboard, 95–100
  list of, Pacific, 16, 17
  purpose of, 93
  unit of United States Navy, 93
Air-battle force pool, 224, 251
Air control, in wartime, 279
Air liner, 133
Air power, 282, 283
Air regulator, 246
Aircraft carriers (*see* Carriers)
Airplanes, flying from carriers,
  formations, 190–192
  types of, 189, 190
    (*See also* individual names)
Air-speed meter, 40
Alaska, 43, 94
Albuquerque, New Mexico, 233, 236, 239, 242, 244, 245, 248
Aleutian Islands, 93
Allegheny Mountains, 234, 235
Altimeter, 40
Amarillo, Texas, 233, 239–241
Anacostia, D. C., naval air station, 214, 223–228
Andrews, Rear Admiral Adolphus, 279
Annapolis, Maryland, 162
Antigua, Guatemala, 94
Army air base, 28, 29
  forts in Hawaiian Islands, 178
Army Air Corps, 280
Asbestos man, 202
Atlantic fleet, 213

B

Balloon hangars, 37, 74, 97
Bases, shore, 190

"Battle lights," 146
Battle wagon, 130
Battleships, 121, 190
Beacons, 232
  rotating, 97
Beam (*see* Radio beam)
Béarn, carrier, 52, 275
Belgium, 276
Belly tank, 197, 199, 200, 201
Black fleet, 136, 137, 144, 162, 163, 167
Blackout, 145, 147
Blind flier, 225
Boat-patrol planes, 185, 186
Boeing planes, 40, 153
Bomb release, 256
Bombers, 36, 114, 189
  light-attack, 130
  long-range patrol, 16, 36, 37, 94
Bombing, 57, 254
Bombing attack, horizontal, 143
Bombing planes, 189, 190
Bombing practice, 66
  (*See also* Dive bombing)
Bombs, 185, 190
Border Field, 16, 63
"Bouncer drill," 80, 81
Breather pipes, 242
Brest, 52, 186, 187, 275, 276

C

Cabrillo, 20
California, flagship, 188, 206
Camera gun, 121
Camouflage, 281
Canal Zone, 30, 36, 94
Carburetor, 244
Carrier, aircraft, 11, 31, 41, 46, 95, 120, 190
  approach to, 60
  cruises on, 103, 120, 125–188
  landing on, 63, 77–82
    first, 102–113
    practice, 16, 38, 101, 145
    thousandth, 109, 114
  signaling airplanes from, 74–82
  unit, 189
Chart board, 138
Check flight, 227
Chief petty officers, 85
Civil aeronautics, 133
Close formation, 192
Coast patrol department, North Island, 29
Coco Solo, air base, 185
Code, reports in, 138
Columbus, Ohio, 233, 235, 237
Combat patrol, 40

Combat work, aerial, 257
  maneuvering, 47
Commandant's reception, 67–71
Compass, 238, 245
Cone of silence, 153, 154
Conferences, before squadron flights, 17–19, 169, 192, 193, 224
Consolidated Aircraft Corporation, 185
Consolidated Flying Boats, 281
Consolidated patrol bombers (PBY's), 177
Consolidated trainer, 78
Control tower, 220, 230, 232
Coronado, California, 27, 28, 249, 260
Coronados Islands, 103, 104, 127–130
Correspondence study, 72, 109
Corrigan, Douglas, 246
Cowl flaps, 113, 131, 143
Cowling, 86
Crack-ups, 46–53, 60, 87, 158–162, 179, 180, 224, 261
  causes of, 46, 47
Crane hoist, 34
Crankshaft, 116
Crash detail, 202

Crashes (*see* Crack-ups)
Crete, 279
Cross-country flying, 163, 231–252
Cruisers, 120, 125, 137–144, 190, 222
Cruises, on airplane carrier, 135–147
  short, 257
Cuba, 204
Curtiss, Glenn, first seaplane flight, 29, 36
Curtiss planes, 277
  pursuit planes, 280
"Cut" signal, 75, 77, 98
CV's, 142
Cyclones, 102, 142, 238

D

Destroyers, 94, 102, 121, 125, 164, 165, 177, 250
  plane guard, 104, 106, 107
Dial settings, 230
Diamond Head, 177, 178, 188
Dive bombers, Martin, 47
  sold to French, 275
  speed of, 190
Dive bombing, night formation, 258
  practice in, 17–23, 96, 138, 140–143, 252

Dive bombing, section formation, three planes, 258
   stationary target, 16
Dive-bombing squadron, 189
Divers, 33, 53
Diving, 174, 282
   vertical, 255, 256
Dogfights, 258
Douglas planes, 277
   torpedo planes, 130, 171
"Duty" calls, 39–43

E

"E" ("Efficiency"), 254–256
Earhart, Amelia, search for, 43
East Coast bases, 223
Eastern Air Lines, 133
Echelon, 18, 20, 105, 142, 173
   definition of, 190, 191
Efficiency, 254, 266
"Emergency, unlimited," 278
Emergency fields, 232
Emergency release, 196
Engineering division, 13, 84
Engines, 31–34, 85, 86, 116, 181, 197, 230
Engine checks, 169

England, 258, 283
Enterprise, carrier, 188, 193, 214
Esprit de corps, 115, 219
Experiment planes, 228, 229
Eye-test machines, 55

F

Fairfax Airport, 237
Ferry trips, 223–226, 231, 243, 252
Fighter planes, 114, 130, 153, 226, 283
Fighting squadron, 189
"Fish," 169
Fixed gunnery, 63, 252
Fleet maneuvers, 158–188, 214
Flight-deck fire stations, 136
Flight division, 13, 84
Flight-quarter stations, 136, 169
Flight school, North Island, 29
Floodlights, 102, 264
Flotation bags, 8, 42, 164
Flotation release, 41
Floyd Bennett Field, commissioned naval base, 279–282
Flying, cross-country, 163, 231–252

"Flying bomb racks," 185
Flying field, main, at base, 16
  outlying, 15, 16
Fog, 60, 196, 201
  flying in, 148–157
Formation, close, 192
  V, 103, 148, 190, 212, 258, 281
Formation flying, 47, 57, 66, 102, 140–158, 190, 192, 204
Formation lights, 258
Forts, Army, in Hawaiian Islands, 178
France, 52, 53, 186, 187
  Navy, 275
  pilots, 276, 277
French Frigate Shoals, 43, 172, 174, 175, 185
Frequencies, 232
Fuel, 41, 88, 164
Fuel-tank selector, 260
Fuel tanks, 195, 198
Fuselage, 199
Fuselage and wing shop, 34

G

Gas gauge, 59
Gas selector, 231
Gasoline, 195, 199, 233, 250

Golden Gate Bridge, 192, 195, 204
Gorgonio, Mount, 89
Groove, 74, 75, 77–79, 107, 133, 201
Grumman amphibians, 6, 7, 37, 76, 115, 129
Guam, air base, 185
Gunnery, 57, 254
  department, 84
  fixed, 63, 252
  practice, 89, 119

H

"Hack," 62, 63
Hangar flying, 43–45
Hatbox, 198, 199
Hawaiian Islands, 30, 36, 94, 167–188
Headrest, 230
Heavy (torpedo) bombers, 190
Heavy-bombing and torpedo squadron, 189
"High Hat" squadron, 220
Hispano-Suiza motor, 187, 276
Holland, 276
Honolulu, 46, 72, 106, 174–188
Horizontal bombing attack, 143

"Hotshots," 97, 98, 129, 216, 220
Hydraulic pressure, 199, 200

I

Ice, 244
 in carburetor, 53
Immelmann, 174, 253
Imperial Desert, 17, 87, 149, 248
Indicator, 33, 198
Instrument board (panel), 114, 122, 230
Instrument flying, 56, 150–152
Instruments, aircraft, 32, 33, 234, 238, 239, 241, 260
 checking, 250
Interphones, 59, 213
"Island," superstructure, 134

J

Japanese fishing boats, 184
Johnston Island, 167, 175

K

Kahoolawe, island of, 176
Kansas City, Missouri, 233, 236, 238

Kauai, island of, 176
Knifing cans, 198

L

Lafayette Escadrille, 219–221
LaGuardia, Fiorello H., 279, 280
Laguna Mountains, 87, 88, 248
La Haina Roads, 144, 166, 174
Lanai, island of, 106, 175, 176
Landing (*see* Carrier)
Landing gear, 114
 switch, 195, 196
Landing light, 143
Landing signals, 74–81, 108, 133
Leave periods, 223, 224
Leper colony, Molokai, 175
Levasseur P. L. 7's, 275, 276
Lexington, carrier, 11, 38, 63, 76, 103–105, 127–129, 196–201, 208
 cruise, 64, 119, 133–188
Life raft, rubber, 7, 42, 86
Light-attack bombers, 130
Light-bombing squadron, 189
Lindbergh, Charles A., 30, 246

Lindbergh Field, 150
Line to switch, 199
Loma, Point, 20, 88, 104, 125, 250
Long-range patrol bombers, 16, 36, 37, 94
Looping, 174, 253
Lost plane, search for, 86–93
Loud-speaker, ship, 111, 139
Loyalty, in the service, 83, 115–118
Lufberry circles, 281
Luftwaffe, 283

M

Machine guns, 86, 95, 96, 185
Mail planes, 178
Maneuvering, methods of, 191, 192
Manifold, 111
Maps, 88, 89, 233, 243, 244
Marine Corps, 24, 25, 61, 62, 94, 103
  Juniors, 67
  planes, 269–273
  target practice, 269
Martin dive bombers, 47
Mary Ann, rescue boat, 33, 34
Mass nonstop flights to Hawaii and Canal Zone, 30, 186

Maui, island of, 99, 106, 144, 174–176
Mechanics, airplane, 32, 36, 197, 198, 238–242, 251, 270
  school for, North Island, 29
Mexicans, 104, 268
Mexico, 16, 28
Microphones, 108, 151, 196, 199, 200, 201
Midway, air base, 175, 185
Mitchel Field, 280
Mixture control, 240
Mohawk Mountain Range, 115, 116
Molokai, island of, 106, 175, 176
Movies, 35, 145, 246, 248

N

National defense, total, 214
Naval Reserve, 274, 278
Navigation division, 13, 84
Navigation instruments, 43
Navy, air base (*see* Air base; North Island)
Navy juniors, 67, 68
Navy Medical Corps, 55, 56
Neutrality patrol, 279, 281
New Mexico, battleship, 193
New York, 204, 280
Night carrier approaches, 74
  landings, 102, 261

Night flying, 74–76, 102, 258–265
Night formation dive bombing, 258
Niihau, island of, 176
Nonstop flights to Hawaii and Canal Zone, 30, 186
Norfolk, Virginia, 185, 223, 229, 276
North Island (San Diego) Naval Air Station, 1–46, 54–103, 125–135, 153–155, 212–226, 263–277
 place in protection and defense, 94, 95
Nova Scotia, 94

O

Oahu, island of, 176–178
Ocatilla air base, 17
Oceanside air base, 16
Oil, temperature, 111
Operations, 226, 227, 251
Otay air base, 16
Overcast, solid, 56–62
Overhaul shops, 31, 32, 102
Oxygen, 179

P

Pacific air force, 16, 17, 30
Pacific fleet, 204, 204, 206, 213
Pacific fleet, President's inspection of, 205–208
Palm Springs, 248
Palomar Mountain, 86, 87
Palomar Observatory, 250
Panama, 43, 93
Panama Canal, 204
Parachutes, 35, 41, 116, 117, 122–124, 160, 161, 228, 230
 packing, 35
Paris, 72, 73, 275, 277
Patrol planes, 30, 221, 222, 281
 bombers, long-range, 16, 36, 37, 94
 mass flights, 186
PBY's (Consolidated patrol bombers), 177
Pearl Harbor, 177, 178, 183–186
Pennsylvania, battleship, 206
Pensacola, training station, 1, 14, 24, 26, 36, 39, 40, 65, 73, 109, 208, 213
Pilotless plane, 272
"Pipe-stem" hookup, 179
Plane-guard destroyers, 42, 104, 106, 107, 160, 170, 188
Planes (*see* Airplanes)
Plotting boards, 127, 137
Plougastel, 187

Post, Wiley, 246
Post office, 36
Practice parades, 192, 193
Practice schedule, 223, 224
Pratt and Whitney engines, 133
Preheater, 53
Propeller, 116, 250
Propeller pitch, 230, 240, 260
Protective patrol, 146
Push-over dives, 253

R

Radio, 18, 20, 48, 58, 90, 92, 94, 142, 150, 154
  code, competition, 266, 267
  practice, 95
  communications, 168, 169, 254
  intercockpit, 168, 169
  testing, 230
  weather reports, 239, 240
Radio beam, 40, 232, 244, 245
  flying on, 57, 150, 152, 155, 156
  frequency, 230
Radio and Communications division, 13, 84
Radio masts, 236
Radioman, 137, 240

Ranger, carrier, 126, 134, 136, 144, 145, 166, 169, 170, 180, 188, 193
Recreation, 266
Regulations, 56, 57, 63, 69
Rendezvous, squadron, 138, 146, 159, 190, 193
Repairs, 34, 94
Reserve tank, 88
Richthofen's Flying Circus, 219
Rip cord, 124
Rockwell Field, North Island, 28, 29
Rolling, 143, 174
Roosevelt, Franklin D., 278
Rotating beacon, 97, 155
Rules (*see* Regulations)
Running lights, 258–260

S

Safety belt, 143, 244, 270
Safety net, 108
Salton Sea, 248
Samoa air base, 185
San Clemente Island, 59, 61–63
San Diego, California, 10, 27, 86, 87, 149, 150, 155, 167, 185, 224, 250, 260
San Diego Bay, 94, 121, 212
San Francisco, 121, 192, 203, 204

San Marcos air base, 16, 17
San Pedro, 121
Saratoga, carrier, 126, 134, 136, 188, 193
Saw, 199
Schedule, practice and maneuvers, 223, 224
Schofield Barracks, 178
Scouting planes, 16, 130, 138, 145, 163
  bombers, 121
  squadron, 140, 189
Seaplanes, 101
  first flight, 29
  French, 186, 187
Search for crashed plane, 86-93
Seattle, 36
Section leader, 259, 262, 264
Security watch, 96
Service store, ship, 35, 36
Sick bay, 54-56
Sights, 121
Signal officer, 261
Signals, landing, 74-81, 108, 133, 201
Silver Strand, 28, 81
Single-plane circle, 133
Single-seater fighting planes, 36, 189, 225, 226
Sitka, Alaska, air base, 30, 185
Skid, flying in, 152
"Sky taxi," 78

Slip stream, 201
Smith, Commander Don, 280
"Smokers," 169
Snyder examination, 55
Social life at air base, 65-74
South Bay, San Diego, 28
Spads, 220
Spanish Bight, 4, 27, 29, 81, 129, 249, 251
Spencer, Lieutenant E. W., 29
"Spirit of St. Louis," 30
Spitfires, 121
Spraying of airplane, 34
Squadrons, comprising unit, 189
  flights, 17-24
  rendezvous, 138, 146, 159, 190, 193
"Squirrel case," 174
Stabilizer, 230
Starter flag, 111
Subinstrument board, 117
Submarines, 94, 163, 187, 275
Sunnyvale, California, 29
Survey gang, 124
Swimming pools, 54

T

Tachometer readings, 111
Tail diving, 18

Target, bombing, 96, 254, 255, 262
sleeve-gunnery, 95, 96, 101, 104, 253, 269-271
towed, 257
TBD's (Douglas torpedo planes), 130
Teamwork, 274
Telescope sights, 19
Tennis, 54
Test flight, 227
Test pilot, 275
Test and supply bases, 214, 229
Theater, station, 249
Tijuana, 268
Timing, split second, 46
Torpedo planes, 37, 169
three-place, 114, 130, 164, 190, 276
Torpedo squadron, 189
Torpedo stations, 136
Tow plane, 254
Towers, Admiral, 280
Tracers, 254, 257
Trinidad, 94
Turn-and-bank indicator, 40
TWA air lines, 133
Two-place planes, 189, 190

U

Utah, battleship, 18, 47, 49, 51

V

V formation, 103, 148, 190, 212, 258, 287
Vought bombers, 19, 161, 171, 277

W

Waikiki Beach, 177, 181
Wake Island, air base, 106, 185
Wands, lighted, for landing signals, 74-81, 108, 133, 201
War games, 158-188, 206, 214
Warm-up check, 137, 138
Wasps, 102
Wave-off flag, 111, 113
Weather forecasts, 235-238, 247, 251
Weather plane, 101
Western Hemisphere, defense of, 28
Wheeler Field, 178
Wheels, 195, 196, 198, 230
White fleet, 136, 137, 144
Wichita, Kansas, 233, 237-239
Winslow, Arizona, 245, 247
Wobble pump, 197

Y

Yeomen, 226-228
Yount (Alexander) Hotel, 181
Yuma, Arizona, 116, 149, 150

8002 92